Legal Issues for Library and Information Managers

William Z. Nasri
Editor

Routledge
Taylor & Francis Group
LONDON AND NEW YORK

First published 1987 by The Haworth Press, Inc.

2 Park Square, Milton Park, Abingdon, Oxfordshire OX14 4RN
52 Vanderbilt Avenue, New York, NY 10017

Routledge is an imprint of the Taylor & Francis Group, an informa business

First issued in hardback 2019

Legal Issues for Library and Information Managers has also been published as *Journal of Library Administration,* Volume 7, Number 4, Winter 1986.

Library of Congress Cataloging-in-Publication Data

Legal issues for library and information managers.

Includes bibliographical references.
1. Library legislation —United States. 2. Librarians —Legal status, laws, etc. —United States.
I. Nasri, William Z.
KF4315.L44 1987 344.73'092 87-4 347.30492
ISBN 0-86656-591-4

ISBN 978-0-86656-591-2 (hbk)

Legal Issues for Library and Information Managers

CONTENTS

Professional Liability 141

William Z. Nasri

Professional liability is based on breach of duty in violation of a standard of professional care. The fact that information professionals have not been sued to date does not negate their potential liability. Any organization's board of directors and its professionals and staff are jointly liable for their actions and/or omissions whether the latter are based on malice or ignorance. Precautions and liability insurance are discussed as possible safeguards against professional liability in libraries and/or information centers.

Legal Issues for Library and Information Managers

Introduction

Libraries and information centers are no different from any other place of work. Library and information management, regardless of the type of service, is equally rigorous and demanding. Many decisions have to be made and invariably they have certain legal implications. Most of these implications are serious and far reaching.

Managers in general and library and information managers in particular, are not trained specifically to foresee legal consequences of their decisions or to safeguard against them. Nevertheless, managers are responsible for all decisions made within the scope of their positions as supervisory staff, middle management or chief executives. Regardless of the fact that ignorance of the law is not an acceptable excuse; the legal issues involved in management are numerous, complicated and entail liability.

The Editor, an educator in the field of library and information management with a background in law, became interested in the legal aspects in management in general and in decision making in particular. The issues involved were discussed with some colleagues and as a result a new course "Legal Issues in Information Handling," was introduced in 1976 at the School of Library and Information Science, University of Pittsburgh. This course is the first and probably the only course of its kind and scope to be offered, as far as the Editor knows, in any school of Library and Information Science. However, in considering a book on the subject, a dimension of practical experience and in-depth treatment of some of the legal issues involved in the management of information services was necessary, from the initial stage of acquiring the information, to the final stage of disseminating it. Authors whose expertise, in each of these stages, was practical as well as profound, were selected and invited to contribute to this effort. With the help of these authors this compendium of articles became a reality. In general, the objective of this publication is to fill the above mentioned gaps in our field and increase the effectiveness of information managers by providing them with a better understanding of certain legal concepts and legal rights and obligations in addition to a clear explanation of potential legal consequences and the means possible of safeguarding against them.

For example, censorship is a legal issue which the field has struggled with for centuries. Library and Information professionals are known to stand firm against any form of censorship. The freedom to read and to acquire knowledge is a part of our constitutional rights in their broader sense. William North, a well known attorney in Constitutional Law who has served as ALA legal counsel for several years, covers censorship in his article and suggests a strategy of defense against the censors in our field. His strategy is broad and adaptable in its application to any environment or function.

On the other hand, acquiring information from the files of the Federal Government is not an easy task. A practical and illustrative article on the subject is provided by Richard M. Schmidt, Jr. and Robert Clifton Burns, two attorneys who specialize in the Public Information Act. They detail the provisions of the act and suggest procedural steps to obtain federal information, including the possibility of acquiring classified material.

Freedom of information is at odds with individual privacy. In the information profession, privacy can be seen in relation to two groups of individuals. The first group affected by privacy represents the users of the informational resources whose reading habits and borrowing records must be protected if the freedom of choice is to be preserved. Anne Marie Falsone, President of Falsone Management Consultants, who has served for ten years as Colorado State Librarian, discusses in her article the privacy of circulation files and provides practical suggestions in dealing with privacy laws. She was also instrumental in the passage of Colorado's confidentiality of Literary Records Act, which is considered a prototype for similar acts in other states. The second group affected by privacy are the employees, who work for a library and or information center and whose personnel records must be kept in confidentiality. James Ledvinka, a professor of personnel management at the University of Georgia reviews in his article the laws that govern access to employees' records, discusses significant court decisions in relation to the topic and makes recommendations for management action.

In dealing with personnel, a manager needs to know the why, what and how of affirmative action. James Jones, a professor of law at the University of Wisconsin at Madison, who was among those responsible for drafting the Affirmative Action Policy, provides an analytical treatment of the Act and sheds light on historical events that led to the establishment of this important legal concept in our society.

Equally important are the Civil Rights Act and other similar acts that address employment discrimination, a matter of vital concern to library and information managers. Mary Hutchings Reed, an attorney who also serves as legal counsel to the American Library Association, surveys in her article, relevant court decisions against libraries in relation to employment discrimination and makes practical suggestions for the library and information managers concerning hiring, discharging and disciplining employees.

Collective bargaining and the increasing emphasis on its role in the work environment both in the public and private sectors, is of equal importance. Gwendolyn S. Cruzat, a professor of Library Science at the University of Michigan who conducts seminars on the topic and who has served for several years as Chairperson of ALA Ad-hoc Committee on Collective Bargaining, discusses in her comprehensive article the history and present status of unionism in our field and concludes with practical recommendations to managers.

Of enduring importance and concern to library and information managers is the legal concept of Copyright and its impact on information services. This concern has been complicated by technological advances. The Editor, as an expert in the area, reviews in his article the provisions of the U.S. Copyright Law as it relates to our field. He shares with the reader his years of experience reflecting on these provisions, and discusses the state-of-the-art in addition to present and potential issues.

Arthur Levine, an attorney specializing in computer law and who serves also as legal counsel to OCLC, expands on the question of copyright as it relates to computer software and data basis. His article should be of help to information managers in comprehending this complicated and still developing area of the law.

Acquiring an automated system in a library and information center is not an easy task to negotiate. Diane Becker, a systems analyst and designer, explains in her practical article the facts that a manager needs to keep in mind. She provides also a check-list of the important points which one needs to examine and consider when negotiating the acquisition of a system.

An issue of potential concern to information professionals in general and public librarians in particular is the "Public Lending Right" (PLR) a legal concept which is at present enforced in several European countries. The issues it raises are serious because the concept was a subject of several consecutive bills in the US Senate, which are attempting to study the feasibility of adopting PLR in the USA. Dennis Hyatt, the law librarian at the University of Oregon and an authority on the subject, discusses the issues that need to be resolved before implementing such a concept. Examples from the other countries are provided for comparison.

Finally, "Professional Liability" is becoming an issue of concern with the rising tide of litigation and the rising cost of insurance. The Editor discusses in his article the possibility of liability in our field, its elements and how to safeguard against it.

It is obvious, that this publication does not attempt to cover all the legal issues involved in library and information management. It includes, however, what the Editor believes are the important issues at the time of this writing. The several contributions which constitute this work are intended to simply explain these issues in a practical way and to heighten the sensitivity of the information managers to their serious nature and obligation.

In the meantime, the reader must keep in mind that the authors' contributions and suggestions in this publication reflect only the authors' informed opinion and do not constitute legal advice nor should they be relied upon in lieu of legal counsel. The reader should seek advice from his/her attorney who is familiar with the reader's particular situation and the facts about it.

William Z. Nasri, JD, PhD
Editor

Legal Issues for Library and Information Managers

A Citadel Under Siege: A Strategy Against the Censor

William D. North

In the sixth century, a monastery was founded at Scyllacium on the sole of Italy's boot to preserve the classics, Christian and pagan. In the shadow of Rome's decline and fall, it kept the light of learning lit. In the dark ages to come, it preserved enlightenment. In a world gone mad with bigotry, illiteracy and atrocity, it saved the past for the future.

The Monastery at Scyllacium is gone but its tradition lives on in the library—which preserves the classics for all men for all time—a storehouse of learning open to all who would open their minds.

There are barbarians in every time and every place who, like the Vandals who sacked and raped Rome, will destroy all they cannot understand or appreciate. These are the barbarians who feel threatened by things new and different; who find comfort only in conformity and security only in orthodoxy; and who are prepared to exorcise by fire the "devils" of treason, heresy and obscenity which they discover in ideas alien to their experience or culture.

In the experience of the library and academic community, these barbarians take the name of "censor." They are the ones, if allowed access to literary works, who are prepared to expunge, expurgate and excise; they are the ones, if allowed access to library shelves, who are prepared to purge, pillage and commit to the pyre; they are the ones, if allowed access to library personnel, who are prepared to coerce, cow and condemn library professionals.

There is no hope that like the barbarian tides of Vandals, Goths and Vikings, the tide of censors will ebb with their education and assimilation

---

William D. North, JD (Harvard), is a Chicago attorney and the Executive Vice President of the National Association of Realtors (NAR). He has served previously as the Association's General Counsel and Senior Vice President. Before joining NAR, he was a partner in the Chicago law firm of Reuben & Proctor, specializing in trade association, anti-trust and constitutional laws. He served also for over 15 years as General Counsel for the American Library Association and for the Freedom to Read Foundation. He also served as President of the Foundation during 1983 and 1984. In addition, he was Counsel to the Special Library Association, American Association of Law Librarians, and was General Counsel of the Center for Research Libraries.

into the societies they invade. Each generation of censors has a vitality of its own which defies accommodation; a vitality born of bigotry, arrogance or fear which permits no integration into a pluralistic society and admits no intercourse with contrary cultures. As the barbarians closed the marketplaces of the ancient world and the trade routes supplying those markets, so the censor would close the marketplace of ideas and the communication channels by which they are supplied.

The result of the barbarian invasions was feudalism; a closed economy, a closed society, a closed marketplace and serfdom. The result of a successful invasion by the censor is intellectual feudalism; a closed mind, closed shelves, a closed marketplace of ideas, and intellectual serfdom. Feudalism, whether political, economic, social or intellectual, always substitutes parochialism for pluralism and prescription and proscription for freedom of choice.

The library has often and aptly been described as the institution most essential to the survival of intellectual freedom. This is because the first and foremost task of the library is the collection and preservation of knowledge, and knowledge, if it can be preserved somewhere, can ultimately become the source of intellectual renaissance everywhere.

But for the library to survive as a storehouse of knowledge, it must also be a citadel capable of defending itself when attacked or besieged by the censor. It must have the bulwarks and ramparts, the weapons, the guardians, and sources of reinforcement to prevail against surprise onslaughts or wars of attrition. Most of all, for the citadel to survive there must be a strategy of defense which utilizes all available resources in a coordinated, consistent and controlled manner.

The development of this strategy of defense and its implementation, the building and maintenance of bulwarks and ramparts, the recruiting and training of the guardians, the stocking of the arsenal and the establishment of sources of reinforcement and relief are all tasks for the library administrator. Only the administrator has the authority and perspective to integrate these components and ultimately only the administrator has the power to command what needs to be done.

TASK NUMBER 1: BUILDING AND MAINTAINING THE BULWARKS AND RAMPARTS

If the library is a citadel, then its bulwarks and ramparts are the written policies by which it:

1. Selects the materials it acquires for its collection; and
2. Determines who may have access to those materials and the terms and conditions of such access.

These policies, when clearly articulated and widely disseminated, are the walls which will first blunt the charge and charges of the censor. Where such policies exist, the censor must first tear them down to gain access to the library collection and if they have been well constructed and maintained this can be a costly, time consuming and usually futile effort.

Library policies like walls must have no "holes" in them; that is, they must be comprehensive. To be comprehensive, the materials selection statement should consider:

First, the service policy of the library. This policy should involve a thorough analysis of the groups the library seeks to serve and the objectives of such service. The groups should be carefully defined in terms of their demographic characteristics as well as their needs and interests. Likewise, the service objectives of the library should be precisely defined not merely in terms of the organic documents establishing the library (charter, law, bylaws, budget) but also in terms of the special priorities it identifies for itself.

Second, the environment in which the library is to function. Environmental considerations will determine, for example, the extent to which the library must "stand alone" or can integrate with other nearby collections; or the extent to which the library will be expected to support academic institutions, local businesses, or professional or cultural groups in the area. These determinations in turn will heavily influence the orientation of selection.

Third, the specifications of the collection. These specifications determine essentially the scope and depth of the collection and are particularly relevant when library resources are limited relative to the breadth of service policy or environment. Collection specifications represent the point of greatest vulnerability to censorship attack and, hence, this rampart of the citadel must be built of policy containing the greatest depth of detail, the highest level of clarity, and the most skillfully constructed criteria for evaluating and reevaluating materials.

Finally, the current selection needs. The selection of materials to satisfy current needs is also a highly vulnerable rampart. It is in cutting off additions to the library collection that censors can be most effective because it is at this point that the library is most vulnerable, economically and legally. Books seeking access to a library collection do not enjoy the same protection as books once they have entered the collection. For this reason, too, the gateway to the citadel must be well defended with detailed and fully justified criteria by which current materials can be objectively identified and their acquisition rationalized.

No matter how well constructed the ramparts of library policy, they still must be maintained to withstand the censor. Maintenance means using them and documenting the fact of such use. Policies which are violated, circumvented or ignored are undermined and will fall like the walls of Jericho when challenged.

The library administrator must assure that a well constructed library selection policy is created and in place; that it is reviewed, revised and extended to encompass every dimension of the library collection; and that it is strictly enforced and observed. Only then will the guardians of the citadel have a rampart from which they can conduct their defense.

TASK NUMBER 2: RECRUITING AND TRAINING THE GUARDIANS

If a library is a citadel, then its guardians are the men and women charged with responsibility for its operation. These include, of course, the library, professionals and the support staff. But they also include the library trustees or directors, as well as the library attorney.

The library administrator has a very special role and responsibility in the recruiting and training of the guardians of his citadel. This is so because the guardians present special problems in terms of loyalty, commitment and morale.

The problem of loyalty rests in the fact that every person possesses some of the instincts of a censor and therefore the very guardians of the citadel against censorship may very well be censors in disguise. The censor in the guise of a library employee can make the citadel impossible to defend. By ignoring selection criteria, he can discredit their existence; by substituting his own criteria, he can, through self-censorship, pervert the collection or restrict its circulation or use.

The censor in the guise of a library trustee or director represents an even more formidable danger. While the "self-censoring" librarian erodes the collection over time, the library trustee or director has the capacity to surrender the collection intact and instantly for purge or pyre.

Likewise, the censor in the guise of library attorney can counsel surrender of legal defenses against which the censor could not possibly prevail.

The library administrator's problem in the commitment of the guardians of the citadel rests in the fact that the capacity to resist the pressure of censorship assault can test the breaking point in almost any person's dedication to intellectual freedom. Such assault can, and frequently does, threaten job, reputation, and even family; it can, and frequently does, involve harassment, litigation, and public ridicule. The censors, like the barbarians of yore, show no quarter in victory or defeat.

The library administrator's problem of morale rests in the fact that the guardians of the library are invariably in a defensive posture. In the nature of things, they must await the assault, bear the brunt of the charge, and never assume the offensive. They must endure not only the dangers of the fight but also the frustration of knowing that there is no final victory but only another peril.

Because of these problems of loyalty, commitment and morale, the library administrator must be particularly sensitive to the attitudes of his staff and to his own example. As regards the issue of loyalty, he must insist upon an understanding and acceptance of the Library Bill of Rights as the price of employment; he must establish procedures by which to identify self-censorship activities on the part of librarians and support staff; he must assure that all staff are trained to understand what censorship is, how it can be identified, and why it is an anathema to library professionalism.

Likewise, the library administrator must take action as regards the library trustees and directors to make them understand the incompatibility of censorship with the responsibility for the governance of the library. Each trustee and director must become individually acquainted with the Library Bill of Rights as well as all other policies of the library governing the selection, collection and dissemination of library materials. Moreover, they should be requested or, preferably, required to subscribe individually to such policies so that disloyalty can never be disguised as mere ignorance.

Finally, the library administrator should, if possible, have legal counsel separate from any organizational or governmental unit with which the library may be affiliated. Where this is impossible, the library administrator should have the power to obtain special counsel where, in the administrator's opinion, his regular counsel may be subject to a conflict of interest or may lack the background or expertise to fully and adequately advise the administrator and its governors of their legal rights to resist censorship challenge.

As regards the issue of commitment, the library administrator can expect commitment only if commitment is given. While some librarians and even some library trustees and directors are prepared to accept martyrdom in opposition to censorship, such sacrifice cannot be expected or demanded. But, the level of commitment required for an effective defense can be expected and demanded, if the library is prepared to commit its resources and reputation to the defense of the people who implement and administer its policies.

The library administrator must be prepared to defend its staff to the community; to respond on their behalf to the media; and to resist political compromise of legitimate library policy. The library administrator must man the battlements and risk the censor's fire side-by-side with his staff. And most of all, the librarian must not be offered up as a sacrifice to appease the censor not only because the censor can never be appeased, but more importantly, because such sacrifice would foreclose all further commitment to oppose him.

As regards the issue of morale, the library administrator must provide positive reinforcement of the concept of "preparedness as a deterrent to censorship." Observance of the procedures, criteria and policies of the library must be given importance and rewarded; deviation from them must likewise be recognized and punished. Like "war games" make military training relevant as a test of preparedness, so the library administrator should, from time to time, cause the conduct or decisions of staff to be challenged by persons both within and outside the library so that the procedures for response to censorship activity can be activated. Morale may be maintained only by making meaningful the effort involved in preparedness. Routine must be interrupted before it becomes mindless rote and boredom must be cured before it produces complacency.

TASK NUMBER 3: STOCKING THE ARSENAL

The library's arsenal must be well stocked to withstand the censor's attack. It is the library administrator's task to assure that the defenders of the citadel have the range and type of weapons they require.

The most important weapon the administrator can provide is a comprehensive complaint processing procedure. The value of such procedure is two-fold:

First, it blunts the speed of the censor's attack by establishing timetables for the consideration of his complaints which permit the library guardians to mobilize, survey and shore up their defenses and seek reinforcements. The blitzkrieg of charges, accusations and demands is deprived of its momentum and much of its terror by the requirements of "due process."

Second, the procedure channels the attack and limits the issues which must be defended at one time. As a consequence, the strength of the censor, his objective and even his strategy can be more effectively identified and the panic, so frequently produced by a multi-front offensive, can be avoided.

A second important weapon in the library's arsenal is legal action under the First Amendment. Such action can be initiated in the form of a petition for declaratory judgment confirming the legitimacy of the selection procedures or criteria or a suit for violation of Constitutional guarantees. The availability and utility of the legal weaponry of the library depends greatly on the availability and resourcefulness of the library attorney. But, properly used, it is the ultimate weapon against censorship.

Yet a third weapon which is highly effective against a censor's terrorist attacks on staff is the employment contract which protects the library administrator and those library professionals supervising the selection and dissemination of library materials. The employment agreement can provide economic safeguards and a job description which will inhibit, if not foreclose, efforts to compel the library staff to censor as the price of continued employment.

Yet a fourth weapon is documentation of selection decisions likely to generate censorship attack. Such documentation should include objective critiques from recognized literary commentators and selection lists. Moreover, it should identify the value of the materials in terms of the library's collection and current needs. Documentation provides not only "early warning" of censorship dangers but also the ammunition required for legal action should that ultimate weapon need to be used.

TASK NUMBER 4: ESTABLISH SOURCES OF REINFORCEMENT AND RELIEF

No citadel can long survive if left to defend itself with only its own resources. The economic, political and social power of the censor can usually overwhelm the library, if not by storm, then by siege and attrition unless reinforcements and relief are available. One of the first strategies of every censorship assault is to isolate the library and its staff and governors from sources of community and media support.

For this reason, one of the most important tasks of the library administrator is the establishment of sources of reinforcement and relief in the media and the community. As important as this task is, it is the one most frequently overlooked until it is too late. It is all too easy for the administrator to take for granted the library's claim to the support and good will of the community; it is all too inconvenient for him to take the time required to acquaint the press with library selection policies, procedures and their vulnerability to the censor; and it is too often too tedious for him to identify and organize the users and friends of the library so that they may be called on for help in a censorship crisis.

Yet, time after time the educated media, the organized users and friends, and the informed community have turned the censorship tide.

So too has the organized library profession when called. Through the Office of Intellectual Freedom of the American Library Association and the associated Intellectual Freedom Committees of State Library Associations, the power, influence and resources of the library community can be brought to the aid of embattled libraries or librarians anywhere. Further, the will of library trustees and directors to resist censorship pressures can be strengthened by the support of the American Library Trustees Association. And, where the censorship battle escalates into litigation, the Freedom to Read Foundation as well as a variety of other defenders of First Amendment rights, are prepared to join the fight on behalf of the library.

Reinforcement and relief is available but it can arrive in time only if its summons is made part of the mobilization plan for the library's defense.

A SUMMING UP

There is risk in analogy. Carried too far, it becomes a contrivance, clever rather than credible. Yet through analogy it is possible to describe the unfamiliar in familiar terms and give ephemeral concepts a reality otherwise unobtainable.

The analogy of the library confronted by a censor's attack with the ancient citadels of learning beset by barbarians is not, in the author's opinion, a mere contrivance. There is need for libraries and librarians to recognize their vulnerability and conduct themselves accordingly.

We are not entering an era of less censorship. Rather, the author believes that the information age will increase the vulnerability of the storehouses of knowledge to attack. For if knowledge is power, as it must be in an information society, then power vests in those who can capture and control the storehouses of knowledge and the channels by which their resources are disseminated.

Truly, today, as in the sixth century, the barbarians are abroad and are seeking once again to parochialize and feudalize our intellectual lives.

Whether they succeed or not will depend, in no small measure, on the willingness and ability of library administrators to "preserve the classics, Christian and pagan" and defend their "citadel under siege."*

*A detailed battleplan for the defense of Intellectual Freedom and the library can be found in the *Intellectual Freedom Manual* published by the Office for Intellectual Freedom of the American Library Association. That document more than any other provides the "know how" and "how to" required to develop the policies, procedures and practices which represent the ramparts and weaponry of the library's defense. From the Library Bill of Rights which establishes the grand strategy of censorship defense to its statements on Labeling, Expurgation, Sexism and Racism in Library Materials, Reevaluating Library Collections, Restricted Access, Confidentiality of Library Records and other applications of such strategy, the Manual is indispensable.

The Freedom of Information Act: An Overview for Librarians

Richard M. Schmidt, Jr.
Robert Clifton Burns

"Access Professionals" – at first glance that phrase might be thought to be a reference to professional librarians. It is not; it is instead a bureaucratese for a group of civil servants within federal administrative agencies. Access Professionals are government employees who administer each agency's response to requests directed to that agency under the Freedom of Information Act (FOIA). The word "access," however, is significant insofar as it suggests a common purpose between the professional librarian and this particular government employee: professional librarians are, after all, primarily concerned with public access to information.

Normally the information reposes within the stacks of a particular library. The FOIA expands the accessible store to the files of all federal administrative agencies. Thus, the professional librarian should have every interest in understanding the possible uses of FOIA when assisting researchers and other library users and when establishing library collection. This article will examine illustrative uses of the FOIA, the scope of information available under the Act, the procedures for obtaining information from government agencies, and important current developments.

POTENTIAL USES OF THE FREEDOM OF INFORMATION ACT

It is clearly understandable why individuals and business concerns subject to regulation by a federal agency, may have an overwhelming interest in access to the files of that agency. However, a large group of library users – historians, authors, academicians, investigative reporters, consumer activists – have an equally significant, if less obvious, interest.

For example, in the late 1970s, historian Alan L. Fitzgibbon began to investigate the disappearance of Jesus de Galindez, a Basque exile who

---

Richard M. Schmidt, Jr., JD, and Robert Clifton Burns, JD, are partners in Cohn and Marks, 1333 New Hampshire Avenue, N.W., Washington, D.C., and serve as counsel to the Association of American Publishers, Inc., and the American Society of Newspaper Editors.

was then living in New York City and teaching at Columbia University. Galindez was an outspoken critic of the regime of dictator Rafael Trujillo, head of state of the Dominican Republic until 1961. In addition, it also appears that Galindez was an FBI informant, supplying information on Spanish exiles. In March, 1956, Galindez was last seen after a student dropped him off at a subway station. Colleagues and commentators alleged that Galindez had been kidnapped and executed by the Trujillo regime. The Trujillo regime countered that the disappearance was engineered by Communist-sympathizers in order to discredit the regime. The subsequent discovery of the body of an American pilot in the Dominican Republic gave rise to allegations that the pilot had been involved in the kidnapping of Galindez.

Fitzgibbon devoted several years to research by traditional methods in his explorations of the Galindez affair. In 1979 he commenced an FOIA action in federal district court against the FBI and CIA, both of which had investigated the case. In 1983, the court ordered both agencies to disclose numerous documents previously withheld from the public by both agencies.[1] Although Fitzgibbon has yet to publish the result of his findings, one can anticipate that, given the extent of the disclosures, his study will cast significant light on U.S. foreign policy toward the Dominican Republic, even if it does not provide definitive support for the thesis that the Trujillo government kidnapped and executed Galindez.

Other academics have made similar use of the FOIA. Columbia University sociology and history professor Sigmund Diamond used the Act to investigate government surveillance of college professors during the McCarthy era.[2] Three labor law professors used the Act to obtain data which served as the basis for their ground-breaking study which effectively discredited most of the behavioral assumptions which served as a foundation for federal regulation of union representation elections.[3] Reporters for a national magazine used the FOIA to obtain portions of the "Rowe Report," which detailed the U.S. Attorney's investigation of allegations that Rowe, an FBI informant posing as a Klu Klux Klan member, actually fired the bullet which killed the civil rights activist, Violet Liuzzo.[4] Finally, the authors were involved in FOIA litigation against the Navy on behalf of a journalist seeking documents concerning the disappearance of the submarine Scorpion in the late 1960s. The disclosed documents led to a widely publicized article which suggested that the probable cause was the on-board explosion of a defective torpedo which had become accidentally activated during a routine testing procedure.[5]

Not all FOIA requests require resort to litigation in order to produce the desired information. The Postal Service, for example, has a comprehensive digest of administrative decisions under the mail fraud statute which may be obtained by, and only by, a formal FOIA request. The authors were able to obtain without litigation the factual materials relied on in a unique decision by the Federal Communications Commission to permit substantial foreign ownership of the parent corporation of broadcast stations even though the Commission's published opinion (less than two pages) provides no factual support for the decision.[6] These materials were refused after informal contacts with Commission staff but were promptly supplied after the FOIA request was filed.

Numerous categories of information in government files of interest to academics, journalists, and lay researchers can be envisioned. NASA, for example, undoubtedly has numerous files and documents available through the FOIA which may prove useful in the current political, and the ultimate historical, assessment of the Challenger tragedy.[7] A comprehensive history of the Civil Rights movement would be impossible without the use of the FOIA to obtain documents from the Department of Justice, the FBI and other federal agencies.

The Congressional Research Service of the Library of Congress under the direction of Dr. Harold C. Relyea has made a compilation of media notices on disclosures made pursuant to the Freedom of Information Act from 1972 through 1984. That compilation includes 439 disclosure accounts and includes material released under the FOIA that appears in 128 books and monographs.[8] Dr. Relyea stated in testimony before Congress that research for the report also found that the FOIA had been employed not only to produce literary biographies, but also artistic works – dramas about physicist Robert Oppenheimer, actress Jean Seberg, and former public official Alger Hiss. It has been used as well to reopen trials and to reinterpret scientific research.[9]

Obviously, then, a library professional providing assistance to a researcher or compiling a collection of related materials for use of future researchers should consider whether the FOIA might be a useful tool. When approaching such a task, the inquiry should focus on whether any government agency had an interest in the subject and might have kept a file thereon. A collection of materials relating to a contemporary author who was a political activist would not be complete without an FOIA request directed to the FBI. For example, the FBI, under court order, released to the American Civil Liberties Union files showing that the Bureau, under the personal direction of J. Edgar Hoover, kept secret files on Helen Keller, Felix Frankfurter, Upton Sinclair, and Clarence Darrow.[10]

SCOPE OF INFORMATION AVAILABLE

All federal administrative agency records must be made available upon request unless they fall within one or more of the nine exemptions set forth in the Act.[11] Before considering these exemptions, the scope of the agencies covered by the obligation must be delineated.

At the outset, "agency" is confined to agencies of the executive branch; the courts and the Congress are excluded. Within the executive branch, the agency must be an independent agency, not one whose sole function is to advise and assist the President. The line is difficult to draw for quasi-public entities which are federally chartered and receive federal funds. The legislative history makes clear that Amtrak, the Postal Service, and the Postal Rate Commission are covered whereas the Corporation for Public Broadcasting is not.[12] The decision as to whether such an entity is an agency is made on a case-by-case basis and focusses on the degree of government control over the entity.[13] However, even if there is some doubt as to whether an entity is covered, a request should be made anyway since the entity may itself be unclear as to its status and might comply with the request.

The nine exemptions to the FOIA are the following categories of information:

1. Legitimately "classified" information (e.g., "Top Secret" documents);
2. Internal personnel rules and practices;
3. Information specifically exempted by other statutes;
4. Trade secrets and privileged commercial information;
5. Inter- or intra-agency memoranda that embody the agency's deliberative process;
6. Personnel and medical files;
7. Investigative reports compiled for law enforcement purposes (but there are exceptions, to be detailed, to this exception);
8. Audit files prepared for regulation of banks and other financial institutions; and
9. Geological data concerning wells.

A detailed elucidation of these exemptions is beyond the scope of this article. The trade secret exemption, for example, is invoked many times in situations where a business concern is seeking information about its competitors and their customers, manufacturing processes, and financial data. It is doubtful that a library professional would become involved in such a request. Several of the exemptions are more likely to come into play in the requests of librarians, researchers and historians.

Research concerning American foreign policy, for example, may often involve FOIA requests directed to the CIA. The Galindez research, previously mentioned, is an illustration. Naturally, the covert nature of CIA operations resulted in the classification of all or part of the agency's documents, bringing Exemption 1 into play. State Department and military documents are often classified as well.

Exemption 1, however, does not permit the government to shield information from public view simply by the liberal application of its "Top Secret" stamp, or even the less restrictive "Confidential" stamp. The document must be properly classified pursuant to defined standards which require that disclosure "reasonably could be expected to cause damage to the national security."[14] The CIA and other agencies have sometimes classified information not because of national security reasons but because of potential domestic political repercussions and courts have often, upon a review of these documents in chambers, ordered their release.

In the Galindez case, for example, the CIA classified documents that revealed that it played an intermediary role in arranging for the return of certain of Galindez's files in the possession of the New York Police Department to Basque government officials. "The deletions made to protect this type of information," the Court said, "appear to be tailored more to prevent public criticism over the CIA's past actions in the United States itself . . . than to guard against disclosures that may inhibit its ability to deal with [foreign intelligence services] in the future."[15]

Government agencies will often classify information that has been publicly disclosed. In the Scorpion submarine case, for example, the Navy classified and withheld portions of the Navy Court of Inquiry, which investigated the submarine's disappearance, even though the classified testimony had been given in open session with numerous reporters present. Many courts have shown a willingness to require disclosure of that type of information.[16]

Exemption 7, which protects investigative reports of law enforcement agencies, will often come into play as well in scholarly and academic research. The FBI, in the Diamond case, relied on that exemption to support withholding documents relating to its domestic surveillance of college professors during the McCarthy era.[17] However, the exemption, by its terms, permits withholding only to the extent that disclosure of the records would (a) interfere with enforcement proceedings, (b) deprive a person of a fair trial, (c) constitute an unwarranted invasion of personal privacy, (d) disclose the identity of a confidential source, (e) disclose investigative techniques or (f) endanger the safety of law enforcement personnel. These "exemptions to the exemption" result in the availability of a wide range of useful information in the files of federal law enforcement agencies. Once an investigative file has been closed, large portions of that file become available for public disclosure. The Court in *Diamond* suggested that at a minimum the FBI would have to disclose the names of academics who had been investigated. In many instances the FBI informers' identity, where they were now dead or had consented to disclosure, would have to be revealed.[18]

PROCEDURES FOR OBTAINING INFORMATION UNDER FOIA

Once it is determined that government files may contain documents of value to research or library collections, the procedures for requesting information under the FOIA is relatively simple. This section will detail the steps involved in making such a request and the various responses to agency replies.

The procedure is set in motion by a simple letter. An example of such a letter is reproduced in the Appendix to this article. The letter should be addressed to the agency officer specified in that agency's regulations as found in the current Code of Federal Regulations. If you do not have access to the Code, it is in most instances sufficient to address the letter to the "Freedom of Information Officer."

The letter should specify in as much detail as possible the information requested. If you are aware of specific documents, cite them in your request. Try to specify a limited time frame for which the documents are requested.

Under the Act, you may be required to bear the costs of research, retrieval, and reproduction of the requested documents.[19] Thus, the letter should set forth the maximum amount you are willing to pay. In the case of requests for academic or scholarly research, these fees may be waived, so you should state the purpose of the request and should ask for such a waiver. The Act does not require disclosure of the identity of the requestor or the requestor's purpose, but the likelihood of waiver increases with both disclosures. Any particular expertise of a requestor should also be set forth in support of the waiver.

Under the Act, the agency has ten days upon receipt of the request to comply. In the case of voluminous or widely scattered documents, the agency may, upon notice thereof to the requestor, obtain an additional ten days. In practice, these time limits are rarely complied with. Both the CIA and the FBI have substantial processing backlogs.

The requestor's remedy is to treat the failure of the response as a denial of the request and, without further administrative appeal, the requestor may institute court proceedings to compel disclosure. Even then, however, the Court has the option to retain jurisdiction and permit the agency further time to collect and reproduce the documents.

In some instances, courts have held that filing suit may move the requestor up in the processing line, but other courts have held that the agency must continue to use a "first-in, first-out" standard notwithstanding the suit.[20] Thus, requestors should be expected to provide some latitude to the agency regarding the time limits and delay instituting suit until their patience is exhausted.

When the agency ultimately responds to the request, it is the rare case where the agency does not withhold some responsive documents and delete portions of the documents disclosed. The cover letter with the documents will set forth the exemptions relied upon to justify the deletions and the withholding of documents. The letter will set forth the requestor's right to an appeal, the time limit in which such an appeal may be filed, and the person to whom the appeal should be addressed. If no time limit is specified, the agency's regulations published in the Code of Federal Regulations should be consulted.

Thereafter, the requestor should file an appeal within the specified period. The appeal need be nothing more than a letter which simply asserts that the withholding is not justified under the specified exemptions and requests disclosure of the withheld documents. In many instances, even such a "bare-bones" appeal letter will result in the disclosure of more material. Consultation with a lawyer may assist in the development of arguments which will give the appeal greater force. The agency has twenty days to respond to the appeal. These time limits are often adhered to more closely, but the same considerations governing agency compliance with time limits for initial responses govern here.

If a complete set of documents is not disclosed, the requestor may institute litigation in federal district court. Obviously, at this point the involvement of an attorney is essential. Attorneys' fees may be recoverable if the suit results in the disclosure of any of the previously withheld documents. This may be the case even if the documents were produced voluntarily by the agency and not as the result of an explicit court order.[21] However, a fee award is by no means mandatory, and an FOIA plaintiff should be prepared to bear attorneys' fees.

CURRENT DEVELOPMENTS

In April, 1985, the Supreme Court held that the CIA need not disclose its sources of information even though the source did not expect or require confidentiality.[22] That case involved a FOIA request to determine the identity of domestic researchers and institutions which participated in chemical warfare and brainwashing tests funded by the CIA. In some instances the programs involved the administration of hallucinogens to unwitting and unconsenting human subjects, two of whom died as the result of overdoses.[23] Obviously these domestic researchers and institutions stood in a quite different position from foreign intelligence sources who might be endangered or become useless should their identities be revealed. The court's holding was that the CIA could withhold identifying any source regardless of the terms under which the information was given.

More disturbing to the professional researcher is the next step taken by the court: in order to protect sources of information, the CIA may also shield "the subject matter of the Agency's research efforts."[24] Thus, the CIA need not disclose under the FOIA that it engaged in research that involved the administration of hallucinogens to unconsenting human subjects in the 1950s. This is a troubling, indeed shocking, result, and it remains to be seen whether lower courts will expand the Court's statement to a blanket exemption of the CIA. The Court might be narrowly read to be saying that subject matter may be shielded only if in fact the source will also *necessarily* be revealed.

The CIA had over the past few years requested a blanket exemption from the Freedom of Information Act despite the fact that as admitted by former CIA Director Admiral Stansfield Turner in an appearance before the 1980 convention of the American Society of Newspaper Editors, the CIA has never lost a case in the courts where it claims that material was classified and therefore should not be released. The CIA subsequently modified its request to ask for an exemption of reviewing "operational files" and Congress did pass legislation granting the CIA such a limited exemption.[25] This exemption still leaves open files of historical interest.

Legislative efforts have been made in the past few years to modify the Freedom of Information Act. In the view of the press groups, public interest groups and other heavy users of FOIA these proposals would make it more of a shield for government than a sword for the public.

Let us all remember the words of James Madison enshrined on the building of the Library of Congress bearing his name: "A popular government, without popular information or the means of acquiring it, is but a prologue to a farce or tragedy; or perhaps both. Knowledge will forever govern ignorance; and people who mean to be their own governor must arm themselves with the power which knowledge gives."

NOTES

1. *Fitzgibbon* v. *CIA*, 578 F. Supp. 704 (D.D.C. 1983).
2. *Diamond* v. *FBI*, 532 F. Supp. 216 (S.D.N.Y. 1981).
3. *Getman* v. *NLRB*, 450 F.2d 670 (D.C. Cir. 1971). Their findings were published in Getman, Goldberg & Herman, *Union Representation Elections: Law and Reality* (Russell Sage Foundation: 1976).
4. *Playboy Enterprises, Inc.* v. *Department of Justice*, 677 F.2d 931 (D.C. Cir. 1982).
5. *Landmark Communications, Inc.* v. *Department of the Navy*, No. 84-1465 (D.D.C. 1984). *See also New York Times*, December 17, 1984, A16 (Late City Final Edition).
6. *Banque de Paris et des Pays Bas*, 6 F.C.C.2d 418 (1966).
7. FOIA disclosures have already led to allegations that NASA wasted substantial sums in its dealing with contractors (including paying for a transcontinental flight by a contractor's dog). *Financial Times*, March 18, 1986, p. 6. Documents released under the FOIA have shown that four employees of a company that built fuel tanks for the shuttle were dismissed in 1982 and 1983 for drug use. *New York Times*, March 3, 1986, p. A11 (Late City Final Edition).
8. Congressional Research Services, *Press Notices On Disclosures Made Pursuant To The Federal Freedom of Information Act; 1972-1984: A Compilation* (August 9, 1984), *reprinted in The*

Freedom of Information Reform Act: Hearings on S. 774 Before a Subcommittee of the Committee on Government Operation, 98th Cong., 2d Sess. 703 (1984) (hereafter *Hearings*).

9. *Hearings*, at 702.

10. *Hearings*, at 725. The FBI released to author William Turner files revealing that the Bureau attempted to discredit Turner and his book, which was critical of the FBI, by providing background information to talk-show host Joe Pyne before Turner, a former agent, appeared on television in 1968.

11. 5 U.S.C. § 522(a)(3).

12. H. Rep. No. 876, 93d Cong., 2d Sess. 8-9 (1974).

13. *Rocap* v. *Indiek*, 539 F.2d 174 (D.C. Cir. 1976).

14. Executive Order No. 12356.

15. 578 F. Supp. at 713.

16. *See, e.g.*, *Founding Church of Scientology* v. *NSA*, 610 F.2d 824 (D.C. Cir. 1979); *Lamont* v. *Department of Justice*, 475 F. Supp. 761 (S.D.N.Y. 1979); *Fitzgibbon* v. *CIA*, 578 F. Supp. at 715.

17. *See* note 2 *supra*.

18. 532 F. Supp. at 225-27.

19. 5 U.S.C. § 552(a)(4)(A).

20. *Compare Open America* v. *Watergate Special Prosecution Force*, 547 F.2d 605 (D.C. Cir. 1976) *with Exner* v. *FBI*, 542 F.2d 1121 (9th Cir. 1976).

21. *Church of Scientology* v. *Harris*, 653 F.2d 584, 587 (D.C. Cir. 1981).

22. *CIA* v. *Sims*, 105 Sup. Ct. 1881 (1985).

23. *See Barrett* v. *United States*, 622 F.Supp. 574 (S.D.N.Y. 1985).

24. 105 Sup. Ct. at 1892.

25. 50 U.S.C. § 431.

APPENDIX

LAW OFFICES
COHN AND MARKS

MARCUS COHN	ROBERT CLIFTON BURNS
LEONARD H. MARKS	J. BRIAN DE BOICE
STANLEY S. NEUSTADT	MARK L. PELESH
STANLEY B. COHEN	JILL JOHNSON-PENNINGTON
RICHARD M. SCHMIDT, JR.	DAVID M. RICKLESS
JOEL H. LEVY	—
ROBERT B. JACOBI	OF COUNSEL
RONALD A. SIEGEL	MARTIN I. LEVY
ROY R. RUSSO	JAMES P. JOHNSON[1]
IAN D. VOLNER	—
LAWRENCE N. COHN	[1]MEMBER COLORADO BAR ONLY
RICHARD A. HELMICK	
BRIAN M. MADDEN	
WAYNE COY, JR.	
N. FRANK WIGGINS	

SUITE 600
1333 NEW HAMPSHIRE AVENUE, N. W.
WASHINGTON, D. C. 20036

TELEPHONE (202) 293-3860
CABLE COMAR-WASHINGTON, D. C.

April 9, 1985

BY HAND

[illegible]
OFFICE OF MANAGING DIRECTOR

Mr. Edward J. Minkel
Federal Communications Commission
Room 852
1919 M Street, N.W.
Washington, D.C. 20554

Re: Freedom of Information Act Request

Dear Mr. Minkel

This is a request under the Freedom of Information Act, as amended, 5 U.S.C. § 552. I am writing to request a copy of all Commission memoranda, correspondence, staff reports, and other documents prepared by Commission personnel which were relied upon by the Commission prior to its release of a letter on December 29, 1966 to the Banque de Paris et des Pays Bas. That letter is reported at 6 F.C.C. 2d 418 (1966), and a copy is enclosed for your reference.

In the event that portions of these documents are properly exempt from release, I request all portions that are reasonably segregable. I also request that in the event any material is withheld, you advise me as to which exemption or exemptions are relied upon.

I am prepared to pay reasonable costs for locating the requested file and reproducing it, although if this amount is to exceed $100.00, I would request that you call me and advise me of the anticipated cost. As provided for in the amended Act, I will expect to receive a reply within ten working days.

If you have any questions regarding this request, please telephone me at the above number.

Sincerely

Robert Clifton Burns

Robert Clifton Burns

cc: Fred J. Goldsmith

Privacy of Circulation Files

Anne Marie Falsone

Privacy of library circulation records has been an issue of concern to librarians for many years. Librarians are usually caught between complying with requests for circulation records from law enforcement agents or journalists, for instance, and the library user's right to privacy and the freedom to read. In recent years the State of Colorado had to face this controversial question. The result was the Colorado Confidentiality of Library Records Law, which might serve as an example in this respect to other states in the nation.

One may ask the following question: What significant event occurred on March 30, 1981? The correct answer is that John Hinckley attempted to assassinate President Reagan on that date. Colorado's passage of a confidentiality of library records law was a direct outgrowth of this event.

When Hinckley was arrested, he had a Jefferson County (Colorado) Public Library card in his wallet. Within a short time, the above mentioned library was inundated with requests from news media for a list of all the books Mr. Hinckley had read. At first the staff attempted to deny these requests. However, the county attorney informed the said staff that Colorado's open records law did not exempt library circulation information from disclosure.

The question regarding privacy of patron records had been discussed within the Colorado library community for some time, but it had taken a backseat to other needed legislation. Local librarians were caught off guard by the prospect of having to surrender circulation records to unauthorized persons.

Further consideration of the matter raised even more questions. For example, could a candidate for public office obtain information regarding the reading habits of an opponent? Could groups wishing to "police" public education obtain information about what teachers and principals were reading? The answer to those questions, plus many others, was "yes."

The Colorado library community began a study to determine what legislation existed in other states and how effective it had been in protecting citizen rights to privacy. One thing that became clear was that, although

---

Anne Marie Falsone, MA, MLS, is President of Falsone Management Consultants (FMC), in Denver, CO. Ms. Falsone served as Colorado State Librarian from 1977-1986.

all laws sought the same goal, the actual legislation differed widely from one state to another. Bills which had been introduced in other states tended to fall into three categories: amendments to the existing public records act, revisions of existing library statutes, or separate statutes specifically intended to address the issue of confidentiality of library records.

An analysis of existing legislation did not indicate whether one type of law were better than another in addressing the issue of privacy of library records. Probably the overriding factor in determining how a privacy act should be handled legislatively is the political issue. In some states, there has been a reluctance to amend the public records act, so a separate bill or an amendment to the library law was preferable. Other states have desired to keep all statutes relating to public records within one law. These states have tended to exempt library records within the public records act. Protection under the law does not appear to differ based on the manner in which an exemption was approved legislatively.

THE ISSUES INVOLVED

Where does the public's right to information conflict with the individual's right to privacy? Laws protecting library records from public scrutiny are at the heart of this question. The issue became more urgent with passage by many states of public records acts in the wake of the Watergate scandal. Selection of reading materials has always been a private activity. But, increasingly, computers and information technology have made the protection of individual rights more difficult and the access to information about reading habits more accessible.

Even more basic to the issue of confidentiality of library records is the privileged relationship which has historically existed between librarians and their patrons. The *Library Journal* characterized this as similar to that "between doctor and patient, lawyer and client, priest and parishioner" (Feb. 1, 1976). This theory was expressed in less emotional terms by the New Jersey State Library: "In order for people to make full and effective use of library resources they must feel unconstrained by the possibility that others may become aware of the books they read, the materials they use, the questions they ask. The awareness and the existence of such a possibility inhibits free usage of the library . . ." (*New Jersey Libraries*, March, 1976).

HISTORY OF THE CONCEPT NATIONALLY

In 1939 the American Library Association endorsed a Librarian's Code of Ethics which included the following statement: "Librarians must protect each user's right to privacy with respect to information sought or received and materials consulted, borrowed, or acquired." Later resolutions passed by ALA tended to strengthen that statement. The Policy on Confidentiality of Library Records adopted in 1971 contained the following recommendations:

1. Formally adopt a policy which recognizes records to be confidential in nature;
2. Advise all librarians that such records shall not be made available;
3. Resist the issuance or enforcement of any court order or subpoena until good cause has been shown.

Many librarians adhered to the above guidelines, but problems arose as more and more states passed public records acts. Librarians then discovered that patron and circulation records are public records.

How do librarians solve this dilemma? By the passage of privacy of library records legislation. This remedy has been sought by more and more states. As of this date, thirty-two states have passed such laws.*

The number of states having statutory authority to protect the confidentiality of circulation records has grown dramatically in the last few years. When Colorado's law was passed in 1983, only thirteen other states had such legislation—plus two states which had Attorneys General opinions protecting the privacy of library records. The addition of seventeen states in just three years indicates the seriousness with which the library community views the issue of privacy of patron records. That concern is well founded in light of the proliferation of automated circulation systems in libraries. Such technology makes information about patrons and their reading habits much more accessible than was true with manual files.

The Texas Attorney General issued the following opinion:

> We believe that the First Amendment guarantee of freedom of speech and press extends to the reader or viewer, and protects against state-compelled public disclosure of a person's reading or viewing habits. . . . If by virtue of the First and Fourteenth Amendments, a state has no business telling a man sitting alone in his own house, what books he may read or what films he may watch . . . then neither does the state have any business telling that man's neighbor what book or picture he has checked out of the public library to read or view in the privacy of his home. (*Library Journal*, Feb. 1, 1976)

*Alabama, Alaska, Arkansas, California, Colorado, Connecticut, Delaware, Florida, Illinois, Indiana, Iowa, Louisiana, Maine, Maryland, Massachusetts, Michigan, Minnesota, Nebraska, Nevada, New Jersey, New York, North Carolina, North Dakota, Oklahoma, Oregon, Pennsylvania, Rhode Island, South Carolina, South Dakota, Virginia, Wisconsin, West Virginia.

PRACTICAL SUGGESTIONS FOR LIBRARIANS

The Colorado Library Association sponsored a program on privacy of user records that featured two attorneys and the author of this article. It soon became evident that one attorney favored a loose interpretation of the law, while the other held to a strict interpretation. In a situation where there is no case law to guide attorneys, it is important for librarians to consult with the attorney for their legislative body and seek advice on how the law will be enforced at the local level. This is an instance where legal advice from some other entity will not be of much help in guiding your action. You need to talk with the lawyer who will defend you if an incident ever occurs.

Even without specific legal advice, there is one rule of thumb that can be used in an emergency. Decisions should be based on a knowledge of the privacy law and on "good faith" behavior. If you can prove that you were acting in good faith, then this can provide protection against spurious lawsuits.

School librarians need to know that a federal law supercedes state public records and privacy laws. For example, the federal Family Education Records Privacy Act (FERPA) gives parents access to all school records belonging to their minor children. Therefore, a school librarian could be asked to inform parents about the reading habits of their children, while a public librarian would not have to surrender such information.

Patron records should not be surrendered even to law enforcement officials without a subpoena or court order. This can create a difficult situation if the officer is standing at the circulation desk demanding the information. However, librarians should be aware that they, not the officer, will be liable if release of the information is against the law.

Most confidentiality of library records acts cover all persons who might have access to privileged information. Library directors and their boards should be careful that student aides and adult volunteers are aware of the law in their state. Librarians should include specific procedures for dealing with situations relating to privacy of patron records in library policy and procedures manuals.

SUGGESTED ACTIONS FOR LIBRARIANS

If the reader of this article belongs to one of the eighteen states lacking privacy of patron record laws, then the author would like to recommend that the said reader might contact his/her library association to garner support for passage of such legislation. On the other hand, if the state has existing legislation to protect library records, the reader should familiarize himself/herself with its provisions and determine if it needs any revision to deal with library automation. Speaking of automation, many libraries do not include confidentiality requirements in their "Request for Proposals" to vendors, when they plan for an automated circulation system. If the reader already has an automated system, the reader should check to see if it conforms with his/her state's privacy laws; if not, the vendor can usually make the necessary adjustments to protect the privacy of the data files against unauthorized use.

Since ignorance of the law is not a legally accepted excuse, one's intentional or unintentional actions may result in liability. Therefore, one has to remember, that as librarian, one is responsible for protecting the library patrons from unwarranted intrusion. The author's advice is to take that responsibility seriously and to become informed, and work within the state to support and protect this important right and privilege.

Privacy Regulations and Employee Record Keeping

James Ledvinka

These are litigious times, and much of the litigating is by employees against their employers. Naturally, then, managers are now more interested than ever in employee rights, and particularly in what they can do to avoid being found guilty of violating those rights. One employee right is the right to privacy. This becomes a management concern because of the vast amounts of personal information that employers keep on their employees, much of it in personnel files and other employee records. Managing this information in a way that minimizes legal risks is a challenge for employers.

The problem is exacerbated by the increased difficulty of preventing intrusions into employee records. In part, this increased difficulty is due to computerization of employee records. Unions are particularly concerned with computerization and the increased potential for unauthorized access that computerization brings. Some labor organizations have already begun to fight the introduction of computer technology in personnel record keeping (see Bureau of National Affairs, 1985b).

But technology is not the only issue. While computerization increases the likelihood of privacy abuses, computerized records are not unique in that regard. More important is the growing number of outside requests for information on individual employees. Employers field requests from government agencies, labor unions, other employers, and the news media, as well as from individuals within the organization. Many of those requests raise privacy issues. There are potential privacy problems in situations such as:

– answering requests for reference information on the job performance of former employees

James Ledvinka, PhD (Michigan), is Professor of Management and Psychology and a member of the Applied Statistics section of the Graduate Faculty of Applied Quantitative Studies at the University of Georgia. He is a fellow of the Division of Industrial and Organizational Psychology of the American Psychological Association and a member of the Academy of Management. His major field is personnel and human resource management and he specializes in government regulation of personnel management. He has authored numerous publications in that area and he serves as a consultant to several government agencies and private corporations here and abroad.

- presenting adverse information on an employee during grievance proceedings
- justifying the termination of an employee in an unemployment compensation hearing by presenting information on the employee's misconduct on the job
- answering requests for information on employees from credit agencies
- making adverse observations about an employee in conversations with other employees
- releasing medical information to supervisors or other employees
- releasing medical information to federal health and safety agencies
- allowing unions to have access to employee files

(See Duffy, 1983; Barnes & White, 1985.)

This article reviews some of the laws that affect employee record privacy. A few of those laws are limited to public-sector employment—they offer privacy protection only to those who work for the government, including the employees of public school and public libraries. In general, legal protection of privacy is greater for public employees than for employees in the private sector, and public sector management's compliance burdens are correspondingly heavier. The article concludes with some recommendations for management action, recommendations that can reduce the risk of legal problems in the area. Nevertheless, it is most important to consult with an attorney before undertaking action in this area. The risks of legal challenges are too great for management to operate without legal counsel.

ORIGINS OF PRIVACY REGULATION: THE U.S. CONSTITUTION

Privacy has been a concern in this nation since colonial days. The colonists' helplessness in the face of searches by the king's soldiers and tax agents was one of the problems that led to the revolution. Consequently, privacy protections were written into the Bill of Rights of the U.S. Constitution, and later into the Fourteenth Amendment. Those protections apply to public-sector employees—the Constitution governs government.

In the Bill of Rights, the Fourth and Fifth Amendments offer privacy protection. The Fourth Amendment protects persons against unreasonable searches and seizures, which can be construed to prohibit government from unreasonably searching employee records. The Fifth Amendment protects privacy in two ways. The first is the famous clause that protects citizens against being forced to testify against themselves. This self-incrimination clause can be interpreted to prohibit government from examining incriminating information provided by the individual, possibly including information in personnel files.

The second Fifth Amendment protection is the guarantee of due process of law. This protection was later extended to employees of state and local government with the passage of the Fourteenth Amendment after the Civil War. Due process of law means that individuals have the right to be notified of actions to be taken against them, and also the opportunity "to be heard and to defend in orderly proceedings" (Black's Law Dictionary). This can be interpreted to limit the conditions under which the federal government as an employer can take adverse action against individual employees based on information in personnel files.

While the Constitutional protections do not apply directly to employment in the private sector, the average employee probably does not appreciate the distinction between governmental invasions of privacy and private ones. The damage to employee relations is the same regardless of whether the employer is public or private. Besides, the distinction may be fading anyway. Traditional management privileges are losing ground to an increased willingness of the courts and legislatures to protect privacy against actions by employers in either sector. This is discussed further later (see Barnes & White, 1985).

NATIONAL LABOR RELATIONS ACT

The main effect of the National Labor Relations Act is to *reduce* employee privacy. It does so by requiring employers to release information to a union when that information is essential to the union's role in representing employees. Conceivably, that information could include personal matters. The rationale behind this provision of the Act is that the interests of the individual must at times be subordinated to the interests of the group—in this case the interests of all employees in effective collective bargaining (see Duff & Johnson, 1983). This rationale has governed court decisions since 1956, when the Supreme Court first upheld the union's right of access to data that the employer deems confidential (NLRB v. Truitt Manufacturing Co., 1956).

However, this doctrine of union access to employee records was significantly limited by the Supreme Court in a 1969 case that allowed an employer to refuse the union's request for confidential information on employment test results (Detroit Edison v. NLRB, 1979). Under the *Detroit Edison* rules, the employer can refuse to disclose information when the following three conditions are met:

1. the information is sensitive
2. the union has not obtained employee consent
3. the employer is not intending to frustrate the union's efforts to represent employees

However, later cases indicate that employers can refuse access only under certain conditions (see New Jersey Bell Telephone Co. v. NLRB, 1983; Washington Gas, 273 NLRB N. 20, 1984; OCAWU v. NLRB, 1983). For instance, in the *Washington Gas* case, the National Labor Relations Board rules that the employer failed to demonstrate that its interest in the confidentiality of disciplinary information outweighed the union's need for the information. There were three reasons why the court found against the employer: (1) there was no policy or past practice regarding confidentiality of records, (2) management never informed employees that their records were confidential, and (3) management had freely disclosed other disciplinary information in the past. (See Lehr & Middlebrooks, 1985.) This is one reason for establishing a formal record privacy policy and communicating it to employees, as discussed below.

PRIVACY ACT OF 1974

Concern over privacy was particularly strong during the early 1970s, due in part to incidents such as Watergate and the Daniel Ellsberg break-in. In 1977, a presidential commission issued a report that focused attention on the relative lack of privacy protections in the work environment (Privacy Protection Study Commission, 1977). Those events culminated in the pass of the Privacy Act of 1974 (Duff & Johnson, 1983).

The Privacy Act of 1974 protects federal government employees by giving them several rights (see Rice, 1978):

1. the right to determine what information is being kept on them by their employers
2. the right to review that information
3. the right to correct erroneous information
4. the right to prevent the use of information for any purpose other than that for which it was collected.

There is also a provision that, subject to certain exceptions, no record maintained on any individual may be released without the consent of that individual. The underlying philosophy of the Privacy Act is that any disclosure of private information without the consent of the individual is inherently an invasion of privacy (Duff & Johnson, 1983).

OTHER FEDERAL STATUTES

Among the other federal laws affecting employee record privacy are the Occupational Safety and Health Act and the Freedom of Information Act. Section 8(c)(1) of the Occupational Safety and Health Act (OSHA) states:

> Each employer shall . . . make available . . . such records regarding his activities as the Secretary [of Labor] . . . may prescribe by regulation as necessary and appropriate.

Because of that clause, the courts have allowed OSHA agencies broad access to medical information on employees (General Motors v. Finklea, 1976; E. I. duPont de Nemours v. Finklea, 1977; Louisiana Chemical Association v. Bingham, 1982). This grant of access has caused employers considerable conflict over privacy issues. In the duPont case, the agency had refused to allow the company to delete personal identifying information before releasing the records. When the company asked employees for their consent to release medical records, 631 refused. Employers can easily be caught between government demands for access to records and employee demands for privacy in these sorts of situations.

The Freedom of Information Act, which was passed in 1966, also tends to reduce privacy protections by providing for the release of private information under certain conditions. The purpose of the Act is to increase the public's access to information rather than to keep it secret. In a sense, then, the Freedom of Information Act operates contrary to the Privacy Protection Act. The Freedom of Information Act does contain an exception for personnel files and other private information, but there have been instances when the courts have ruled that the public's right to know outweighs the individual's right to privacy (Department of the Air Force v. Rose, 1976). Here again, employers seem to be placed under conflicting demands with regard to the confidentiality of employee records.

There are a variety of other federal statutes that affect employee record keeping, but only by limiting the kind of information that can get into employee records, not by limiting how information is handled once it gets there. Actually, the major statutory controls over the management of employee record information are not federal laws but state privacy laws. These are discussed next.

STATE PRIVACY STATUTES

Eleven states have passed laws regulating access to personnel files. Some of the state laws protect government employees only, others protect private-sector employees only, and still other protect employees in both sectors. Like the federal Privacy Protection Act, the state laws generally allow employees to control access to their personnel files and correct any misinformation there. Most of them also exempt certain kinds of information: letters of recommendation, security reports on suspected internal conduct, information on future management operations, and the like (Duff & Johnson, 1983).

The state statutes differ in their treatment of access by unions. On the one hand, Pennsylvania prohibits union access, while Michigan and the District of Columbia authorize it. Other states take a middle ground. Connecticut, for instance, prohibits disclosure unless personal identifying information has been deleted from the materials released (Duff & Johnson, 1983).

COMMON-LAW PRIVACY PROTECTIONS

Perhaps more important than statutory protections are common-law protections. Common law is a body of law emanating from court opinions that do not interpret statutes or other legislative enactments. Common law principles derive their authority from judicial decree rather than from legislative action. Those principles are long standing, widely applicable standards of justice that have been passed down from ancient times.

The branch of common law most applicable to employee record keeping is the law of torts. A tort is a wrong or an injury. One form of tort with particular relevance to employee record keeping is *defamation*. In the employee record-keeping context, defamation occurs when the employer discloses false information that tends to injure an employee's reputation. Defamation takes place when the employer purposely or carelessly gives out incorrect derogatory information about the employee (Lehr & Middlebrooks, 1985). The characteristics of defamatory information are:

1. it concerns the employee
2. it is actually publicized or disclosed
3. it is false
4. it damages the employee's reputation
5. the employer's disclosure of it is malicious or negligent

Notice that defamation does not depend on proving that the employer *intended* to defame the employee—it is sufficient to show that the employer simply intended to publicize or disclose the information (Lehr & Middlebrooks, 1985).

The defenses against defamation claims are (1) *truth* and (2) *privilege*. Regarding truth, the burden of proof is often on the employer. If the statement is defamatory, it is presumed to be false unless the employer demonstrates otherwise. The term "privilege" refers to a kind of exemption that the courts grant from liability for defamation. The courts may grant privilege to an employer's communication of private information when the communication:

1. was made in good faith
2. concerns something about which the employer has a legitimate interest or duty
3. concerns something about which the person to whom it is communicated has a legitimate interest or duty (Lehr & Middlebrooks, 1985)

In addition, privilege is ordinarily granted when an employer communicates private information to public officials on a matter of public interest. The idea behind the granting of privilege is that society has an interest in certain kinds of information exchange, enough so that they should ordinarily be presumed legitimate (Duffy, 1983).

However, the privilege granted to an employer regarding the release of an employee's record information is a *qualified* one: it can be withdrawn by the courts if it is *abused*. Among the abuses of privilege that apply to the release of an employee's record information are (Duffy, 1983):

1. *malice:* the intentional infliction of harm without just cause or excuse. Malice can be inferred from unreasonable conduct, such as deliberately communicating false information or, sometimes, being negligent about determining whether it is true or false
2. *excessive publication:* disclosing the information in an overly public manner, or disclosing it to more people than necessary (e.g., posting an employee's discharge notice in a public place)
3. *excessive language:* communicating too much information (e.g., conveying non-job-related information in response to a reference request), or using vituperative language (e.g., using racial epithets in the communication)

Despite the existence of those abuse categories, the courts have been reluctant to limit employer privilege (Duffy, 1983). While the risk of losing defamation suits is a real one, particularly when there is an abuse of privilege, the courts have tended to give employers fairly wide latitude. Nevertheless, employee challenges have been increasing, and the courts' willingness to award damages has also been increasing when the information is inaccurate (Duff & Johnson, 1983).

MANAGEMENT RECOMMENDATIONS

Observers and commentators have offered numerous proposals for management action to prevent legal problems (see Benson, 1978; Rice, 1978; Fox & Ostling, 1979; Bureau of National Affairs, 1985a; Lehr & Middlebrooks, 1985; Barnes & White, 1985). The original report of the Privacy Protection Study Commission (1977) offered the following management suggestions:

1. Limit the collection of information to that which is relevant to specific personnel decisions
2. Give employees access to their personnel records
3. Inform employees and applicants about how their records will be used
4. Allow employees to correct inaccurate information
5. Limit the release of information to third parties without the employees' consent
6. Limit the external disclosure of employee information.

One particularly troublesome area of employee record privacy concerns how to respond to requests for reference information. Because of employee challenges, many employers have instituted policies that severely limit the release of information about former employees to potential employers. Rice (1978) recommends the following steps:

1. Document all information that is released
2. Release specific, objective information only
3. Obtain written consent from employees before releasing information
4. Do not blacklist employees
5. Do not answer the question of whether you would rehire the employee – if your answer is "no," you would not want to be held responsible for the other party taking your advice

The main effect of those precautions is to *objectify* reference information. Objectively verifiable information is more capable of being proven true, and truth is the prime defense against claims of defamation.

Barnes & White (1985) offer some additional recommendations regarding employee record privacy:

1. Review the employment application process to be certain that all the information collected is necessary and relevant to making the employment decision
2. Subdivide the personnel file into separate sections for different per-

sonnel decision-making purposes: performance information, payroll information, medical information, background or general information, and the like. The idea is to make sure that people in the organization do not get information that they do not need. For example, it is unlikely that the payroll office would have any need to know the employee's medical problems

3. Document each piece of information that is added to the file, noting the source, recipient, and date of the information. This can help casual, anonymous information from finding its way into personnel records
4. Establish standard policies for gathering and releasing information, and be certain that each person responsible for the personnel files is familiar with those policies

This last step may be most important of all. Recall that the employer's right to refuse union requests for information generally depends on the existence of a policy or past practice of privacy protection, plus the communication of that policy to employees. Without a coherent policy, the employer may have no legal power to deny requests for information from employee records. Besides, a carefully developed policy will not only help management resist invasions of privacy, but also contribute to a positive employee relations climate by standing as evidence of management concern for the rights of employees to keep personal information confidential.

Library and Information managers face the same aforementioned concerns about the privacy of employees' records. The above mentioned overview and recommendations are as equally applicable to them as to any managers in the private or public sector. They are also equally advised, as mentioned earlier, to consult with their legal counsel before making decisions regarding this highly sensitive area of management of human resources.

REFERENCES

Barnes, T. J. & White, J. P. (1985). Employee privacy rights: "Everything you always wanted to know—but shouldn't," *Michigan Bar Journal*, 1104-1112.

Benson, P. G. (1978). Personal privacy and the personnel record, *Personnel Journal, 57*, 376-380, 395.

Bureau of National Affairs (1985a). Employees' privacy rights, *Employee Relations Weekly, 3*, 816.

Bureau of National Affairs (1985b). Privacy rights, *Employee Relations Weekly, 3*, 1569.

Black's Law Dictionary (1968). (St. Paul, MN: West Publishing Co.).

Department of the Air Force v. Rose, 425 U.S. 352 (U.S. S. Ct., 1976).

Detroit Edison v. NLRB, 440 U.S. 301 (U.S. S. Ct., 1979).

Duff, K. J. & Johnson, E. T. (1983). A renewed employee right to privacy, *Labor Law Journal*, 747-762.

Duffy, D. J. (1983). Defamation and employer privilege, *Employee Relations Law Journal, 9*, 444-454.

Fox, J. C. & Ostling, P. J. (1979). Employee and government access to personnel files: Rights and privileges, *Employee Relations Law Journal, 5*, 67-83.

Lehr, R. I. & Middlebrooks, D. J. (1985). Work-place privacy issues and employer screening policies, *Employee Relations Law Journal, 11*, 407-421.

New Jersey Bell Telephone Co. v. NLRB, 720 F.2d 789 (3rd Cir, 1983).

NLRB v. Truitt Manufacturing Co., 351 U.S. 149 (U.S. S. Ct., 1956).

OCAWU v. NLRB, 711 F.2d 348 (D.C. Cir., 1983).

Rice, J. D. (1978). Privacy legislation: Its effect on pre-employment reference checking, *The Personnel Administrator, 23*(2), 46-51.

Privacy Protection Study Commission (1977). *Personal Privacy in an Information Society* (Washington, DC: U.S. Government Printing Office).

Washington Gas, 273 NLRB N. 20, 1984.

The Genesis and Present Status of Affirmative Action in Employment: Economic, Legal, and Political Realities

James E. Jones, Jr.

INTRODUCTION

It is somewhat difficult to establish a birthdate for affirmative action, but I shall assign one, based on recent history. The *modern* concept of affirmative action *as program* emanates from the United States Department of Labor's issuance of the Philadelphia Plan on June 27, 1969,[1] under Executive Order 11246.[2] That plan was the first attempt by the federal government to require employers in the construction industry to establish goals and timetables for the employment of minorities and women for construction projects financed by the federal government.

Although the term "affirmative action" is relatively modern, its legal and conceptual underpinnings are rooted in the ancient history of Anglo-American law. The older concept is rooted in equity, a higher justice, which originally was a separate body of law administered in England by the Court of Chancery to respond to the undue rigidity of legal rules or the inadequacy of legal remedies.[3] More modern adaptations of flexible and equitable responses to novel problems for which law has provided inadequate solutions are illustrated by the proliferation of independent administrative agencies in the 1930s.[4] A prototype is the National Labor Relations Board. That Board was given jurisdiction with exclusive authority, power to investigate, issue rules and regulations, prosecute, and adjudicate. It is empowered upon a finding of an unfair labor practice to issue cease and desist orders and to take such affirmative action, including reinstatement of employees with or without back pay to effectuate the policies of the National Labor Relations Act.[5]

James E. Jones, JD (Wisconsin), is John Bascom Professor of Law and the Director of the Industrial Relations Research Institute, University of Wisconsin at Madison. He served as the Director of the Office of Labor Management (Policy Division) and as the Associate Solicitor of Labor, U.S. Department of Labor, 1966-69, where he was instrumental in drafting the Civil Rights Policy for the Johnson Administration. He is also the co-author of *Labor Law, Employment Discrimination*, and *Foundations of Equal Employment Opportunity*, in addition to several other publications. This article originally appeared in The Genesis and Present Status of Affirmative Action in Employment: Economic, Legal and Political Realities, 70 IOWA LAW REVIEW (1985).

THE "GENESIS" OF AFFIRMATIVE ACTION

Affirmative action can be defined as public or private actions or programs which provide or seek to provide opportunities or other benefits to persons on the basis of, among other things, their membership in a specified group or groups.

Although the term "affirmative action" is recent, Congress has considered, and approved, laws and programs involving essentially the same issues in previous periods of our history. Early examples of this nation's efforts to address problems of discrimination are illustrated in the legislative history of the Fourteenth Amendment.[6] After the Civil War, Congress adopted a series of race-conscious laws providing a variety of benefits to blacks only. Those laws are an undeniable precedent of the legality and constitutionality of public programs designed to provide special benefits for persons on the basis of their membership in a specified group.

More recent examples of affirmative action in employment may be traced to the executive orders of the Presidents, beginning with the order issued by President Franklin Roosevelt in 1941 in response to a threat by A. Philip Randolph, who was then the President of the Brotherhood of Sleeping Car Porters, to march on Washington to demonstrate against racial discrimination by war contractors.[7] President Roosevelt's response in 1941 resulted in the establishment by executive order of the First Fair Employment Practices Committee (FEPC).[8] Between 1941 and 1961, federal efforts at prohibiting discrimination by private firms that held federal procurement contracts continued this "committee" approach, which consisted largely of voluntary efforts by employers. The final report of one of the last President's Committee on Government Contracts, chaired by then Vice-President Nixon, contains an excellent statement of the problem to be addressed by, and the public policy justification of, affirmative action:

1. Overt discrimination, in the sense that an employer actually refuses to hire solely because of race, religion, color or national origin is not as prevalent as is generally believed. To a greater degree, *the indifference of employers to establishing a positive policy* of nondiscrimination hinders qualified applicants and employees from being hired and promoted on the basis of equality. . . .
2. There is no justification for discrimination in employment because of race, color, religion, or national origin in work performed by contractors paid by federal funds. . . .[9]

Shortly thereafter, the first use of the term "affirmative action" appeared in President Kennedy's Executive Order 10,925 which not only prohibited discrimination on the basis of race, religion, color and national origin, but also required affirmative action to ensure equality of employment opportunity.

LEGAL MEANING OF AFFIRMATIVE ACTION

The last section highlighted that both the legislative and executive branches of our government have addressed and approved "race-conscious" remedies prior to the current era of affirmative action. The judicial branch also has a considerable history in dealing with the same issue. Moreover, it is through this body of case law that the term "affirmative action" acquires a legal meaning. In cases involving jury duty,[10] voting rights,[11] employment[12] and education,[13] the Supreme Court has distinguished between inflexible and illegal quotas and flexible and legal quotas. What we learn from those cases is that a quota is a system which restricts or requires participation of a fixed and inflexible number of ratio of minorities;[14] which involves involuntary imposition of inflexible requirements;[15] which includes sanctions to enforce compliance with the requirements;[16] and in which the relevance of the requirements to the class affected and the evil perceived is questionable or unestablished.[17]

This is to be compared with the modern concept of affirmative action. The Philadelphia Plan involved the establishment of goals and timetables for the utilization of minorities and women. At the beginning the focus was limited to blacks and as such presented a cleaner case for constitutional approval. The government looked at the utilization patterns of blacks in the Philadelphia area, in the counties and trades in question, and determined what "but for discrimination," ought to have been a reasonable level of participation of blacks in the construction trades. The critical aspect of modern affirmative action programs is the requirement of hiring *goals* rather than hiring *quotas*. What was required of the covered contractors was that they *make good faith effort* to achieve a *goal* chosen by them which fell within the approved ranges promulgated by the government.[18] If they failed to make the target they had chosen within a permissible range, the failure triggered an investigation to determine whether they had made a good faith effort.[19] Nowhere is there a requirement to utilize unqualified people. Moreover, the plan, on its face, prohibited intentional discrimination against the white worker in carrying out affirmative action objectives.[20]

Later, when the government wrote general affirmative action rules and made them applicable to nonconstruction contractors of a certain size, it required that the contractor perform his own utilization analysis in order to determine whether the number of protected class participants in the contractor's specific job categories was less than their availability in the relevant job market.[21] Thus, the goals and timetables concept is less governmentally determined than were the Philadelphia Plan and subsequently imposed plans.

By a close reading of the requirements, no fixed quota, no inflexible timetable, and no hiring of the unqualified was imposed by the government. The maximum requirement is a good faith effort to reach targets within time limits both of which involve a substantial degree of choice by the contractor undertaking to perform under the plans or rules.

THE CURRENT STATUS OF AFFIRMATIVE ACTION

Legal Status

Three Supreme Court decisions have substantially determined the constitutionality of affirmative action. *Regents of the University of California v. Bakke*[22] involved a quota program for the admission of nonwhites into a medical school. In that case, the court held that the use of race classifications for purposes of remedial programs or programs of inclusion such as the program at issue in this case was constitutionally permissible. Although the particular program involved was found to be in violation of the law, it provided a clear majority for some use of race as a basis for remedial programs. Mr. Justice Powell, in setting forth how programs could appropriately be crafted using race classifications, made favorable references to lower court decisions in which the Philadelphia Plan concept had been challenged and sustained.[23]

Mr. Chief Justice Burger, announcing the judgment of the Court in *Fullilove v. Klutznick*, noted that it is unnecessary to show that prime contractors are responsible for a violation of antidiscrimination laws in order for the set-aside obligation to be imposed on them.[24] He stated that under Title VII the Court has expressed no doubt regarding the congressional authority to prohibit practices challenged as perpetuating the effects of discrimination occurring prior to the effective date of the Act, if such conduct was not unlawful when it occurred.[25] Noting these powers under the commerce clause, he stated further that under the fourteenth amendment, Congress has additional authorization to deal with the effects of prior discrimination.[26] On examining the means utilized, he concluded that Congress enacted the programs as strictly remedial measures that function prospectively in the nature of an injunctive decree.[27] And he rejected the contention that Congress must act in a wholly color-blind fashion when undertaking such a program.[28] He did make the distinction that this case did not deal with the limited remedial powers of the federal court but with the broad remedial powers of Congress.[29] Nothing is clearer, in a careful reading of this opinion, than the Court's approval of the authority of, indeed the invitation to, legislative bodies and chief executives to deal with these difficult problems of sharing the burdens of past discrimination. The critical significance of Klutznick is the Court's determination that it is not the exclusive province of the judiciary to address the effects of past discrimination.[30] It was thought more appropriate for elected officials, such as chief executives and appropriate legislative bodies, to establish affirmative action programs than it is for the federal judges who are appointed to serve for life during good behavior. Congress continues to enact legislation requiring minority set-asides in contracting.[31] There have also been substantial responses by elected officials at the state and local level to address the issue of past discrimination by affirmative action programs.[32]

Until recently the Supreme Court has refused to review affirmative action cases not arising under federal law.[33] In June 1984 the Supreme Court decided *Firefighters Local Union No. 1784 v. Stotts*.[34] The *Stotts* case involved the authority of the district court to modify a consent decree so that it would override seniority, in order to protect affirmative action hirees from layoffs, when the district court finds that the language of the consent decree does not mention layoffs, and the city, party to the consent decree, opposes the modification.[35] There are two significant issues: first, the question of the content of consent decrees within the four corners thereof; second, the position of seniority as protected under the language of Title VII and the prior ruling of the Supreme Court in *Teamsters v. United States*.[36] In *Stotts* the court of appeals had found that the seniority system was bona fide.[37]

The ultimate conclusion reached in the *Stotts* case was very narrow. The Supreme Court held that a district court does not have the authority to modify a consent decree in a manner that would affect the existing seniority system over the objection of one of the principal parties (the city) where actual discrimination had not been established and where the seniority system was found by the court to be bona fide (that is, it did not illegally continue present effects of past discrimination). Assertions that it was "the most significant case of the decade"[38] have turned out to be vastly overstated. The case certainly did not establish that programs that are *prospective* in impact (such as affirmative action) are illegal.

Even if the broadest interpretation of the dicta in *Stotts* proves correct, it would not affect directly the affirmative action plans about which we principally have been concerned in this paper. The First Circuit contributed an excellent discussion of the two contexts in which affirmative action arises in *Associated General Contractors v. Altshuler*.[39] In the first context courts, pursuant to federal statutes, including Title VII, have ordered remedial action for past discrimination:

> In fulfilling their "duty to render a decree which will so far as possible eliminate the discriminatory effects of the past . . . ," *Louisi-*

> *ana v. United States*, 380 U.S. 145, 154, . . . (1965), courts have ordered unions to grant immediate membership to a number of minority applicants, *United States v. Wood, Wire, and Metal Lathers International Union, Local No. 46*, 471 F.2d 480 (2d Cir. 1973), cert. denied, 412 U.S. 939, . . . (1973); to begin affirmative minority recruitment programs, *United States v. Sheet Metal Workers International Association, Local No. 36*, 416 F.2d 123 (8th Cir. 1969); to match normal referrals with minority referrals until a specific objective has been obtained, *Heat and Frost Workers, Local 53 v. Vogler*, 407 F.2d 1047 (5th Cir. 1969); or to take on a certain number of minority apprentices for each class of workers, *United States v. Ironworkers Local 86*, 443 F.2d (9th Cir. 1971), cert. denied, 404 U.S. 984 . . . (1971). Courts have also ordered employers to hire minority employees up to a thirty per cent of the total work force, *Stamps v. Detroit Edison*, 365 F. Supp. 87 (E.D. Mich. 1973); to hire one minority worker every time two white workers were hired, up to a certain number, *Carter v. Gallagher*, 452 F.2d 315 (8th Cir. 1971), cert. denied, 406 U.S. 950, . . . (1972); and in our own *Castro v. Beecher*, 459 F.2d 725 (1972), we ordered that . . . [minority applicants] for police positions, who had failed to measure up to a constitutionally impermissible set of hiring standards, be given priority in future hiring.[40]

Thus, the first context involves affirmative action directed by a court as an order or *remedy* where discrimination has been established (or the parties have entered into a consent decree). It is in this first context that the *Stotts* case falls.

The second context involves *programs* which have been legislatively or administratively determined necessary by an appropriate public authority. In the second context courts have upheld federal affirmative action programs against challenges under the equal protection clause or under the antipreference provisions of Title VII of the Civil Rights Act of 1964. The *Altshuler* court noted that, "[r]ecognizing that the discretionary power of public authorities to remedy past discrimination is even broader than that of the judicial branch, see *Swann v. Charlotte-Mecklenburg*, supra at 16 of 402 U.S., 91 S.Ct. 1267; cf. *Katzenbach v. Morgan*, 384 U.S. 641, 653, . . . (1966), courts have upheld the specific percentage goals and timetables for minority hiring found in the Philadelphia Plan."[41] The *Altshuler* court further indicated that the use of racial criteria should be subject to strict scrutiny and given legal sanction only where a compelling need for the remedial action can be shown.[42] It did not question that a compelling need exists to remedy serious racial imbalances in the construction trades and that the necessary conditions existed in the instant case to withstand challenge.[43]

Frequently, the distinction is blurred between the first and second affirmative action contexts. In fact, there has been a general tendency over the last decade to ignore the distinction. Sometimes it has been intentional and disingenuous.

Stotts is not the first case in which the Supreme Court has specifically addressed the remedial powers of the federal courts under Title VII. In *Albermarle Paper Co. v. Moody*,[44] the Court discussed the purposes of Title VII in connection with the back pay powers of the district courts and concluded that Congress took care to arm the courts with full equitable powers, for it is the historic purpose of equity to secure complete justice:

> "Where federal protected rights have been invaded, it has been the rule from the beginning that courts will be alert to adjust their remedies so as to grant the necessary relief." . . . Title VII deals with legal injuries of an economic character occasioned by racial or other antiminority discrimination. The terms "complete justice" and "necessary relief" have acquired a clear meaning in such circumstances. Where racial discrimination is concerned, the "district court has not merely the power but the duty to render a decree which will so far as possible eliminate the discriminatory effects of the past as well as bar like discrimination in the future."[45]

The Court again focused on remedial powers in *Franks v. Bowman Transportation Co.*,[46] in the context of the fictional seniority question. The Court limited the facts on review to identified victims of past discrimination.[47] And again, in *Teamsters v. United States*,[48] the Court ruled that competitive seniority could be awarded only when the beneficiary of the award had actually been a victim of illegal discrimination.[49] The *Stotts* decision does no more than apply the Teamsters rationale on seniority relief to a court modification of a consent decree silent on its face regarding seniority and layoffs. It does not address the larger issue of the equitable powers of the courts to grant prospective relief in situations in which discrimination of a more generalized form has been judicially determined and in which barring future discrimination requires a court to fashion remedies which may go beyond relief to identified victims of discrimination.

The Eleventh Circuit recently decided a case involving an attack on an affirmative action program based upon a county ordinance requiring set-asides for minority contractors.[50] The court sustained the program and indicated that it drew the following important standards for reviewing affirmative action programs of this type from *Bakke* and *Fullilove*:

1. that the governmental body have the authority to pass such legislation;

2. that adequate findings have been made to ensure that the governmental body is remedying the present effects of past discrimination rather than advancing one racial or ethnic group's interest over another; and
3. that the use of such classifications extended no further than the established need of remedying the effects of past discrimination. Legislation employing benign racial preferences, therefore, must incorporate sufficient safeguards to allow a reviewing court to conclude that the program will be neither utilized to an extent nor continued in duration beyond the point needed to redress the effects of the past discrimination.[51]

The combination of *Bakke* and *Fullilove* gives sound advice as to compliance with the Supreme Court's edicts. The Supreme Court has agreed to hear three cases involving affirmative action during the 1985 term. As of this writing, the decision in one case has been announced. In *Wygant v. Jackson Board of Education*,[52] a case decided May 19, 1986, the Supreme Court addressed an issue left open in the *Weber* case regarding voluntary adoption of affirmative action plans by public employers. The City of Jackson and its union had negotiated a collective bargaining agreement which not only provided for affirmative action in hiring but protected minority teachers from layoffs. A majority of the Court concluded that the layoff provision was unconstitutional because it was not sufficiently narrowly tailored and because it maintained levels of minority hiring that had no relation to remedying *employment* discrimination. More specifically, the particular plan was invalidated because the hiring goal protected by the layoff "was tied to the percentage of minority students in the school district, not to the percentage of qualified minority teachers within the relevant labor market."[53]

Despite the continued cacophony of opinions from the court it seems that a consensus has emerged on fundamental issues. The focus here is on Justice O'Connor's views. Her vote is necessary to make a majority for disposition of the case, and her opinion states the principles which are supported by a substantial majority of the Court. Justice O'Connor believes that the Court is in accord that "a public employer, consistent with the Constitution, may undertake an affirmative action program designed to further a legitimate remedial purpose and which implements that purpose by means that do not impose disproportionate harm on the interests, or unnecessarily trammel the rights, of innocent individuals. . . ."[54]

The Justice concludes that the Court has rejected the proposition that there must be contemporaneous *findings of discrimination* before an employer may act. Rather "[W]here these employers, who are presumably fully aware both of their duty under federal law to respect the rights of *all* their employees and of their potential liability for failing to do so, act on the basis of information which gives them a sufficient basis for concluding that remedial action is necessary, a contemporaneous finding requirement should not be necessary. . . . Indeed, our recognition of the responsible state actor's competency to take such steps is assumed in our recognition of the state's constitutional *duty* to take affirmative steps to eliminate the continuing effects of past unconstitutional discrimination."[55] Justices Marshall, Brennan and Blackmun believe that the particular plan under attack was constitutional. Justice Stevens, arriving at the point by a different route, also concluded that the plan was constitutional and that the Court of Appeals should be affirmed.

What do we glean from this multiplicity of voices which may be of assistance in determining the status of affirmative action? I suggest a careful reading of the opinions identifies a majority of the court for the proposition that public employers, like private employers under Title VII, may constitutionally adopt affirmative action programs giving certain special status to appropriate minorities. However, those programs must be carefully crafted. They must address the elimination of past discrimination and there must be some record of prior discrimination by the acting entity. Not even the plurality takes the position that the constitution requires color blind action. Justice Powell, joined by Rehnquist and Chief Justice Berger, states that "we have recognized, however, that in order to remedy the effects of prior discrimination, it may be necessary to take race into account. As part of this nation's dedication to eradicating racial discrimination, innocent persons may be called upon to bear some of the burden of the remedy."[56]

It seems apparent from the *Wygant* case that the Justice Department's assertion that affirmative action is limited to granting remedy to identified victims of discrimination has been rejected. Justice O'Conner finds agreement on the Court that plans need not be limited to remedying specific instances of identified discrimination for it to be deemed sufficiently narrowly tailored or substantially related to the correction of prior discrimination by the state actor. The Administration has also contended that Title VII restricts relief to identified victims of discrimination. That position has been rejected overwhelmingly by courts of appeals.[57]

The two pending decisions *(Local 28 and Local 638 of the Sheet Metal Workers v. EEOC* (cert. granted 106 S. Ct. 58 (1985) and *Vanguards of Cleveland v. City of Cleveland* (cert. granted 106 S. Ct. 59 (1985)) provide an opportunity for the Supreme Court to make clear, if clarity is necessary, that section 706(g) of Title VII of the Civil Rights Act also does not restrict relief to identified victims of discrimination, but permits the imposition of prospective relief which includes affirmative action plans.

Preferential treatment programs to remedy past discrimination and imbalances in participation in the bounties of our society are issues of allocation of limited resources between competing, legitimate interests. In a democracy such matters are more appropriately decided by elected offi-

(1) Black employment share increased relatively more in contractor establishments under the affirmative action obligation than in noncontractor establishments between 1974 and 1980. This was true for both males and females controlling for establishment size, growth, industry, region, occupational structure, corporate structure, and past employment share. (2) This positive impact has been relatively greater in the more highly skilled occupations, and has resulted in net occupational upgrading for both male and female blacks. (3) Compliance reviews, the major enforcement tool, have been effective in promoting the employment of male and female blacks. (4) The impact of affirmative action on nonblack minorities and on white females has been mixed. (5) Economic growth plays a key role in bringing minorities and females into the workplace; minority and female employment shares increase faster in expanding establishments. (6) The relative productivity of females and minority males has not significantly declined as their employment share has increased; similarly, changing demographics have not had a significant effect on corporate profits. (7) The success of affirmative action in racially integrating the workplace has been limited by residential segregation, a problem aggravated by the suburbanization of employment. (8) The goals agreed to by contractors under affirmative action are inflated, but those who promise to hire more do hire more minorities and females.[81]

Given our history of virulent racism, it is counterintuitive to conclude that our efforts at counteracting it have had no effect on the situation we now see before us. It seems compelling that the advance by blacks up the occupational ladder, which clearly has started to occur, did not happen by chance. Affirmative action programs obviously need to be continued to assure that progress is not lost. Moreover, the current attacks on affirmative action demonstrate, particularly in periods of economic uncertainty, that minorities who have made it up the occupational mobility ladder continue to need protection. The bottom line in the mosaic of civil rights laws enacted since 1964 is that women, blacks and other minorities are entitled only to their "rightful place." Rightful place is another way of saying they are entitled to a fair shot if there is a vacant job available which they can perform.

Affirmative action is designed to ensure a fair share of available new jobs. It does not deal with problems of economic dislocation, the dwindling of blue-collar jobs, the increase in technology, the greater educational requirements, or a whole host of other factors which affect the economy and the job market.

The Political Scene

When the current Administration first took office, the future of affirmative action was greatly debated, with suggestions that the program would be discarded. There have been criticisms that rather than discarding it, the Administration has returned to yesterday's voluntarism.[82] As of mid-June 1986 the Office of Federal Contract Compliance Programs under the preexisting executive order remains in place.

It has also been suggested that the executive order program was vulnerable to elimination by the President with a stroke of a pen and that in his second term the President would be more disposed to respond to the shrill minority which opposes affirmative action and scrap the program. However, there may be legal problems with the stroke of the pen proposition.[83] I contend that this executive order is virtually unique. There has been such substantial congressional reliance on its continued existence that it is not in the category of prior orders subject to elimination with the stroke of a pen. The original Title VII, and the 1972 amendments, were written in reliance upon the continued existence of the executive order program.[84] The Vietnam Veterans' protections[85] and the government's handicapped initiative,[86] enacted by Congress, were mounted upon the existing contract compliance structure and committed to the Department of Labor's jurisdiction.[87] In 1978 President Carter's Reorganization Plan left those programs with the Department of Labor.[88]

Even during the Reagan Administration, with a Republican Senate and a President on record against "quotas," Congress has enacted legislation which explicitly endorses the existing federal affirmative action requirements imposed pursuant to Executive Order 11,246.[89] Part G of the Job Training Partnership Act is specifically titled "Affirmative Action."[90] These provisions authorize contractors, subject to affirmative action obligations under Executive Order 11,246, to establish or participate in federally funded training programs and to use such participation as evidence of compliance with their affirmative action obligations.[91] This became law on October 13, 1982.[92] It would be hard to find a more explicit statutory adoption of the affirmative action obligations of Executive Order 11,246 than these provisions.[93] More modest protections of affirmative action are contained in legislation dealing with the restructuring of certain railroads. In giving hiring preferences on any other subject rail carrier to certain qualified employees laid off prior to January 1, 1984, the law explicitly excludes from that first right of hire any vacancy covered by "an affirmative action plan, or a hiring plan designed to eliminate discrimination, that is required by Federal or State statute, regulation, or Executive order, or by the order of a Federal or State court or agency, or . . . a permissible voluntary affirmative action plan."[94]

These statutes, and others,[95] were passed and signed into law by President Reagan. Thus, the actions of this administration, unlike some of the rhetoric, indicate adoption of affirmative action. Moreover, these congressional actions make an even stronger case for contending that Executive Order 11,246 is not subject to revocation by a presidential stroke of the pen.

The survivability of affirmative action rests, in my judgment, on the proposition that politicians can and do count even if they do not, or may not be able to, read. Fifty-three percent of the population is female (figures show fifty-six percent of the voting population); close to eighteen percent of the population is nonwhite. Assuming one-half of the nonwhite population is female and thus has already been counted, the result is that sixty-two percent of the population are direct beneficiaries of affirmative action programs. Both women and other minorities are increasingly active today in the political arena. The serious run that Jesse Jackson made for the nomination for the presidency ought to make it clear that sometime in the future a rainbow coalition will become a more significant force in American politics. The nomination of Geraldine Ferraro as the Democratic vice-presidential candidate attests to the rising power of women. Both parties eagerly count the Hispanic vote. I believe any administration would be politically reckless to decide to destroy affirmative action, given the political potential of the affected classes.

CONCLUSIONS

It seems clear from close examination of the economic, legal, and political factors which have contributed to the emergence of the modern affirmative action concept that no cataclysmic event can be identified as the necessary and sufficient cause of its emergence. Historically, the genesis of preferential treatment to an oppressed minority in America is rooted in the reconstruction era efforts of the 1860s. A fair reading of the legislative history surrounding that earlier effort also provides persuasive authority in the constitutionality of affirmative action. If one reads the documents creatively, it is arguable that the underlying concepts existed prior to their explicit enunciation in the executive order of President John F. Kennedy in 1961. Moreover, the link between the Eisenhower Administration's perceptions of principal difficulties, and the response in Executive Order 10,925, are facially clear. What stands out most in this historical or evolutionary examination is that the modern affirmative action concept grew incrementally over the years.

I believe affirmative action is constitutionally secure. As I read the Court, it has put the issue to the political process where in its judgment it belongs. I believe that the body politic and its most accountable representatives, legislative and executive, have accepted the validity of affirmative action for minorities and women, and it is no longer the critical issue. The now and future issue is comparable worth and there seems to be sufficient momentum behind the exploration of this inequity that it will receive even more serious attention in the near future.

It strikes me that the willingness of this society to address seriously problems of the grave nature raised by comparable worth is evidence that our confidence in the fundamental fairness of our system has not been misplaced, yet. It strikes me that any precipitous rejection of the affirmative action theories which we have managed to secure from constitutional threat so recently would send a negative signal regarding confidence in that system. I must in all candor admit that we have seen previously an ebb and flow in the fortunes of civil rights. I can only hope that we have seen the last of retreat from principle.

NOTES

1. For a detailed discussion of the background and legality of the Plan, see Jones, The Bugaboo of Employment Quotas, 1970 Wis. L. Rev. 341, 347-48, 364-73 [hereinafter cited as Jones, Employment Quotas]; Leiken, Preferential Treatment in the Skilled Building Trades: An Analysis of the Philadelphia Plan, 56 Cornell L. Rev. 84, 87-91, 98-112 (1970); Comment, the Philadelphia Plan: A Study in the Dynamics of Executive Power, 39 U. Chi. L. Rev. 723, 724 n.8 (citing numerous other articles on the Philadelphia Plan and affirmative action). 725-32, 739-47 (1972). See also Jones, "Reverse Discrimination" in Employment: Judicial Treatment of Affirmative Action Programs in the United States, 25 How. L.J. 217, 226-30 (1982) [hereinafter cited as Jones, Reverse Discrimination]; Jones, The Transformation of Fair Employment Practices Policies, in Federal Policies and Worker Status Since the Thirties 159, 190-93 (J. Goldberg ed. 1976).

2. 3 C. F. R. 339 (1964-1965 Comp.), reprinted in 42 U.S.C. S 2000e (1982).

3. See D. Dobbs, Handbook on the Law of Remedies 24-45 (1973).

4. See B. Schwartz, Administrative Law 11-14 (1976).

5. See *Labor-Management Relations Act*, 1947, 29 U.S.C., 150 (1982 comp.).

6. See the Brief of the NAACP Legal Defense and Educational Fund, Inc., as amicus curiae to *Regents of the University of California v. Bakke*, 438 U.S. 265 (1978).

7. Exec. Order No. 8802, 3 C.F.R. 957 (1938-1943 Comp.); see also L. Kesselman, The Social Politics of FEPC (1948); R. Weaver, Negro Labor (1948).

8. USCCR Book, supra note 37, at 10.

9. President's Committee on Government Contracts, Pattern for Progress,(1960) at 14 (emphasis in original).

10. See *Bush v. Kentucky*, 107 U.S. 110, 121 (1882); *Neal v. Delaware*, 103 U.S. 370, 397 (1880).

11. 383 U. S. 301 (1966).

12. See *United Jewish Organizations v. Carey*, 430 U.S. 144, 155-56 (1977).

13. 395 U.S. 225 (1969).

14. *Ibid*. at 234.

15. Hughes, 339 U.S. at 461-62, 467.

16. Truax, 239 U.S. at 35.

17. See Jones, Employment Quotas, supra note 8, at 373-78.

18. 41 C.F. R. S 60-2.15 (1984).

19. *Ibid*. SS 60-2.22 to .25.

20. *Ibid*. S 60-2.30.

21. *Ibid*. S 60-2.11.

22. 438 U.S. 265 (1978).

23. *Ibid*. at 301-302.

24. 448 U.S. 448 & 475, (1980).

25. *Ibid*. at 475.

26. *Ibid*. 25 476.

27. *Ibid*. at 481.

28. *Ibid*. at 482.

29. *Ibid*. at 483.

30. 448 US at 472-73.

31. See, e.g., Amendments to the Small Business Act, Pub. L. No. 95-507, S 211, 92 Stat. 1760, 1767 (1978) (current version at 15 U.S.C. S 637(d) (1982) (requiring negotiated contracts in excess of $1,000,000 for construction or $500,000 with regard to other contracts to include a subcontracting

plan providing percentage goals for the utilization of small business concerns owned and controlled by socially and economically disadvantaged individuals; such firms are defined as at least 51% owned or controlled by blacks and/or other minorities); see also Surface Transportation Assistance Act of 1982, Pub. L. No. 97-424, S 105(f), 96 Stat. 2097, 2100 (1983).

32. It no longer appears that affirmative action is a controversial topic for most states. Over half the states have some form of affirmative action program. Eighteen states are working under executive orders. Eleven states have administrative regulations mandating affirmative action programs. Nine states (and the District of Columbia) have passed laws validating and encouraging affirmation action plans. For a complete guide to state laws, see [8(a) Fair Empl. Prac. M.] Lab. Rel. Rep. (BNA). No exact figures are available for cities. Neither the EEOC, OFCC, United States Commission on Civil Rights, nor the National League of Cities keeps a record of how many cities have adopted affirmative action plans.

33. See, e.g., *Tangren v. Wackenhut Services*, 658 F.2d 705 (9th Cir. 1981), cert. denied, 456 U.S. 916 (1982); *Associated Gen. Contractors v. Altshuler*, 490 F.2d 9 (1st Cir. 1973). cert. denied, 416 U.S. 957 (1974); *Weiner v. Cuyahoga Community College Dist.*, 19 Ohio St. 2d 35, 249 N.E. 2d 907 (1969). cert. denied, 396 U.S. 1004 (1970); see also *Morgan v. O'Bryant*, 671 F.2d 23 (1st Cir.). cert. denied, 459 U.S. 827 (1982); *Contractors Ass'n v. Secretary of Labor*, 442 F.2d 159 (3d Cir.). cert. denied 404 U.S. 854 (1971)

34. 104 S. Ct. 2576 (1984).

35. *Stotts*, 104 S. Ct. at 2581-83.

36. 431 U.S. 324 (1977).

37. *Stotts*, 104 S. Ct. at 2582.

38. Will, It Calls a Bluff, Wash. Post, June 17, 1984, at D7, col. 1.; see also Barbash, High Court Rules for Seniority. Not Affirmative Action, Wash. Post, June 13, 1984, at Al, col. 5; Barbash & Sawyer, Justice Dept. Declares Win Over Quotas, Wash. Post, June 14, 1984, at Al, col. 1.

39. 490 F.2d 9 (1st Cir. 1973). cert. denied, 416 U.S. 957 (1974).

40. 490 F.2d at 16-17.

41. 490 F.2d at 17; see also *United States v. City of Miami*, 614 F.2d 1322 (5th Cir. 1980); *Contractors Ass'n v. Secretary of Labor*, 442 F.2d 159 (3d Cir.), cert. denied,404 U.S. 854 (1971).

42. 490 F.2d at 17.

43. *Ibid.* at 18.

44. 422 U.S. 405 (1975).

45. *Ibid.* at 418 (citations omitted) (emphasis added).

46. 424 U.S. 747 (1976).

47. See *Ibid.* at 751-52.

48. 431 U.S. 324 (1977).

49. *Ibid.* at 353-54.

50. See *South Fla. Chapter of the Associated Gen. Contractors v. Metropolitan Dade County*, 723 F.2d 846 (11th Cir. 1984).

51. *Ibid.* at 851-52 (emphasis in original).

52. *Wygant et al. v. Jackson Board of Education*, U.S. Supreme Court No. 18-1340, 122 Labor Relations Reporter, No. 5 (May 19, 1986).

53. *Wygant v. Jackson Board of Education*, ______ U.S. ______, 40 FEP Cases 1321 at 1332 (1986) (J. O'Connor, conc.).

54. *Wygant v. Jackson Board of Education*, 40 FEP Cases 1321 at 1329.

55. *Ibid.* at 1331.

56. *Ibid.* at 1326.

57. See e.g., *Deveraux v. Geary*, 765 F.2d 268 (1st Cir. 1985); *U.S. v. City of Buffalo*, 779 F.2d 881 (2nd Cir. 1985); *Local 28, 638 v. EEOC*, 753 F.2d 1172 (2nd Cir.) cert. granted 106 S. Ct. 58 (1985); *Kromnick v. School District of Philadelphia*, 739 F.2d 894 (3rd Cir. 1984). cert. denied, 105 S. Ct. 782 (1985); *Grann v. City of Madison*, 738 F.2d 786 (7th Cir. 1983). cert. denied, 105 S. Ct. 296 (1984); *Britton v. South Bend Community School Corporation*, 775 F.2d 794 (7th Cir. 1985).

58. See, e.g., Small Business Act, 15 U.S.C. S 637(d) (1982); Surface Transportation Assistance Act of 1982, Pub. L. No. 97-424, S 105(f), 96 Stat. 2097, 2100 (1983).

59. *Ibid.* footnote 32.

60. See 42 U.S. C. S 2000e-17 (1982).

61. Pub. L. No. 95-454, S 310,92 Stat. 1111, 1152 (1978) (codified at 5 U.S.C. S 7201. 1982).

62. See 5 U.S.C. S 7201(b) (1982).

63. Equal Employment Opportunity Comm'n, Seventeenth Annual Report for Fiscal Year 1982, at 36-37 (1983).

64. At almost every meeting on affirmative action, representatives of major corporations who attend or participate indicate no intention to desert affirmative action as a human resource practice. Most recently, on June 14-15, 1984, at the Bureau of National Affairs-Industrial Relations Research Association (D.C. Chapter), representatives of Merck & Company, Du Pont, and the Edison Electric Institute (a 200-member trade association) indicated their intention to continue affirmative action. Additionally, Thompson Powers, EEO partner in Steptoe & Johnson, and T. Timothy Ryan, Jr., former Solicitor of the United States Department of Labor, both of whom currently represent major corporations in Title VII litigation, indicated that they advise their clients to maintain their affirmative action programs.

65. See, e.g., U.S. Comm'n on Civil Rights, Clearinghouse Pub. No. 74, Unemployment and Underemployment Among Blacks, Hispanics and Women (1982).

66. *Ibid.* at 55-57.

67. *Ibid.* at 55.

68. *Ibid.* at 14-27, 55-56.

69. Cain, The Economics of Discrimination: Part I, Focus, Summer 1984, at 1,2 (University of Wisconsin, Madison Institute for Research on Poverty).

70. *Ibid.*

71. *Ibid.*

72. *Ibid.* at 4.

73. *Ibid.*

74. *Ibid.* at 5.

75. See, e.g., Goldstein & Smith, The Estimated Impact of the Antidiscrimination Program Aimed at Federal Contractors, 29 Indus. & Lab. Rel. Rev. 523,523-24 (1976). Heckman & Wolpin, Does the Contract Compliance Program Work? An Analysis of Chicago Data, 29 Indus. & Lab. Rel. Rev. 544,544-46 (1976).

76. See, e.g., Goldstein & Smith, supra note 237, at 529-31, 532-35; Heckman & Wolpin, supra note 237, at 546-48, 555.

77. See, e.g., Goldstein & Smith, supra note 237, at 529-31, 532-35; Heckman & Wolpin, supra note 237, at 546-48, 555.

78. Leonard, The Impact of Affirmative Action on Employment. 2 J.Lab. Econ. 439 (1984).

79. *Ibid.*

80. *Ibid.*

81. *Ibid.* at 446-60.

82. Citizens' Commission on Civil Rights Report, 116 Lab. Rel. Rep. (BNA) 175, 175-76 (July 2, 1984).

83. See Jones, Twenty-One Years, supra note 62, at 117.

84. See Subcommittee on Labor of Senate Comm. on Labor & Pub. Welfare, supra note 98, at 209-10.

85. Viet Nam Era Veterans Readjustment Act of 1974, Pub. L. No. 97-306, 96 Stat. 1436 (codified at 38 U.S.C. SS 2000, 2012. 1982).

86. Vocational Rehabilitation Act of 1973, Pub. L. No. 93-112, 87 Stat. 357 (codified as amended at 29 U.S.C. SS 701, 793. 1982).

87. See Viet Nam Era Veterans Readjustment Act of 1974, Pub. L. No. 97-306, 96 Stat. 1436 (codified at 38 U.S.C. SS 2000, 2012. 1982); Vocational Rehabilitation Act of 1973, Pub. L. No. 93-112, 87 Stat. 357 (codified as amended at 29 U.S.C. SS 701, 793. 1982).

88. 3 C.F.R. 321 (1978 Comp).

89. See Job Training Partnership Act, Pub. L. No. 97-300, S 481, 96 Stat. 1322, 1390 (codified at 29 U.S.C. SS 1501, 1781. 1982).

90. *Ibid.*

91. *Ibid.*

92. *Ibid.*

93. See also 29 U.S.C. SS 1603(a)(l). 1691-1692 (1982).

94. 45 U.S.C. S 1004 (1982); see also id. S 907.

95. See, e.g., 22 U.S.C. S 3905(b)(2) (1982); 23 U.S.C. S 140 (1982; 29 U.S.C. SS 1755, 1781 1982).

Employment Discrimination and Related Litigation in Libraries

Mary Hutchings Reed

On March 7, 1964, five young black men entered the adult reading room of the Audobon Regional Library in Clinton, Louisiana. One requested a copy of "The Story of the Negro" by Arna Bontemps. The assistant told him she would obtain the book from the State Library and mail it to him or he could pick it up from his "point of service" – a bookmobile. The librarian then asked the young blacks to leave; they did not. In ten minutes, the sheriff arrested them "for not leaving a public building when asked to do so by an officer," and they were convicted of disturbing the peace. Three days later, the library obtained the requested book and mailed it to the man who had requested it with a note, "You may return the book either by mail or to the Blue Bookmobile." The United States Supreme Court reversed their conviction in 1965 and noted ironically, "The reference to the color of the vehicle was obviously not designed to facilitate identification of the library vehicle. The Blue Bookmobile is for Negroes and for Negroes only."[1]

Justice Fortas wrote, "It is an unhappy circumstance that the focus of these events was a public library – a place dedicated to quiet, to knowledge, and to beauty."[2] Happily, review of reported cases against libraries since the days of the Blue Bookmobile reveals only a handful of cases in which libraries have been found guilty of discrimination, although the discrimination that is now the focus of judicial scrutiny is far more subtle and the regulatory mechanisms designed to root it out are more complex.

Today, the major legal activity involving librarians encompasses hiring, firing, promoting, and paying of employees. A computerized search on Lexis for labor and employment cases reported since 1965 uncovered 35 cases involving libraries; 17 of these were against the Library of Congress.[3] "Wronged" employees in those cases found a number of federal

Mary Hutchings Reed, JD (Yale), is a partner in the Chicago office of Sidley & Austin, and legal counsel to the American Library Association. She specializes in Intellectual Property Laws and teaches the subject in the graduate Arts, Entertainment and Media Management Department of Columbia College in Chicago.

statutes* under which to seek redress: the Civil Rights Act of 1964 (Title VII);[4] the Equal Pay Act of 1963;[5] the Rehabilitation Act of 1973;[6] the Age Discrimination Act of 1975;[7] and the Age Discrimination in Employment Act.[8] And of course, government employees have found cause to protest firing or promotion decisions under the First, Fifth, and Fourteenth Amendments.

The purpose of this article is neither to exhaust the reader with the legal theories and precedents applicable to employment practices in libraries nor to panic the library administrator faced with difficult employment decisions. Rather, it is to highlight in a somewhat anecdotal manner some particular problem areas. The citation of cases is not exhaustive, merely illustrative.

CIVIL RIGHTS ACT OF 1964

Title VII of the Civil Rights Act of 1964 prohibits employers of 15 or more persons in businesses affecting interstate commerce from making employment, promotion or discharge decisions with respect to an employee's compensation and terms of employment "because of such individual's race, color, religion, sex or national origin."[9] The Age Discrimination in Employment Act prohibits the same discriminatory practices on the basis of age. Because of the broad remedial sweep of these two statutes it is not surprising that libraries have found themselves as defendants in such actions.

Illustrative is the case of *Jackson v. City of Killeen*, decided by the United States Court of Appeals for the Fifth Circuit in 1981.[10] There the plaintiff, a black woman with a bachelor's degree in library science, protested her discharge after only five months of work. Initially assigned to the circulation desk, she was expected to perform a variety of tasks. The library contended in her written notice of dismissal that the reasons for her discharge were: "(a) incompatibility; (b) questioning of assignments; and (c) lack of amenability to counselling."[11]

The Court of Appeals reversed, finding that the library had articulated legitimate reasons for her discharge and that she had not maintained her burden of showing the reasons to be "pretextual" (i.e., assumed reasons in order to cloak the real intention). The Court's opinion succinctly states how a trial of claims like Mrs. Jackson's should progress.

First, the plaintiff must show a *prima facie* (i.e., legally sufficient to establish a case) case by establishing the following elements by a preponderance (i.e., the heavy weight) of the evidence:

---

*In addition, many state and local governments have passed nondiscrimination statutes and ordinances that in some instances provide even greater protections than do the federal laws.

1. that the plaintiff is a member of a protected class
2. who, while qualified for the job,
3. was discharged and replaced with a member of an unprotected class.

On the other hand, the defendant must "articulate some legitimate, nondiscriminatory reason for the employee's rejections."[12] If the defendant can do so, then the plaintiff has the burden of proving that the defendant's articulated reasons are merely pretextual and that the plaintiff's race was in fact a factor that made a difference in the discharge decision.

While Mrs. Jackson could obviously prove that she was a member of a protected class, she could not prove that she was qualified for the job. Her only evidence regarding her competency was her BLS and two years of experience in a junior high school. The library showed, however, through the testimony of three library employees, including her supervisor, that the plaintiff could not type, file, shelve or alphabetize; that others had to redo her work, and that she appeared untrainable. As the court noted, evidence of competence to be hired does not demonstrate actual competence on the job.[13]

PERSONNEL FILES

The *Jackson* case appears to have been a close call for the Killeen library. Perhaps the library should have terminated the employee by means of a letter that specifically identified her job deficiencies so as not to have left open the possibility that her race was the real reason. In fact, the vague reasons set forth in the dismissal letter may have contributed to the plaintiff's desire to sue. In addition, there seems to have been no evidence that her personnel file at the library adequately documented her poor performance. Such a contemporaneous paper record, made prior to a discharge decision, may have strengthened the library's case so that reliance on the oral testimony of three library witnesses would not have been so crucial to the appellate court's reversal.

Libraries must, however, take care not to misuse personnel files. In *Gee v. Boorstin*,[14] the plaintiff, a female black activist, successfully challenged the denial of her promotion to a supervisory position in the Catalogue Publication Division. The United States District Court, in finding for the plaintiff, relied in part on the fact that a special personnel file was maintained on the plaintiff and relied upon by the library in denying the promotion. The file was filled with memoranda from her immediate supervisors, one of whom was accused of deliberately discrediting employees by submitting false statements about their performance.

Obviously, files should not contain references to an employee's political beliefs, since the appearance of reliance on such factors by a public employer can be actionable. For instance, in *Lodico v. U.S.*,[15] a plaintiff contended that the individual responsible for hiring the Chief of the Library Service at Allen Park Veterans Hospital impermissibly relied on information from the plaintiff's previous employer regarding her political beliefs in deciding not to hire her. Summary judgment as to the hiring officer was denied, thus allowing a trial on whether the defendant in fact had been motivated by the plaintiff's political beliefs, or whether the hiring officer would not have hired her even if he had not known of her political beliefs.

There is also a need to clearly articulate the reasons for a hiring or termination decision. In *Mandhare v. W.S. La Fargue Elementary School*,[16] a librarian who was denied reemployment was reinstated after bringing a Title VII suit. The elementary school librarian's contract had not been renewed and she had not been reappointed to an open junior high school position. The librarian, an Asian (Indian), was not recommended for reappointment by her principal because "her heavy accent and speech patterns and grammar problems prevented her from effectively communicating with primary school students."[17] Her principal's review of her performance stated that she did an excellent job of organizing, categorizing and preparing library materials but that she needed to improve her English. He also stated that he believed she "would do an excellent job at a school where her speech and storytelling skills would not be so crucial."[18]

The Court held that the school board's reason for not giving her the junior high school position was a "feigned contention."[19] In essence, the court held that her inability to communicate with *primary* school students was irrelevant to her qualifications for appointment in a *junior high school*. Perhaps an expression of concern over the plaintiff's ability to adequately communicate with young people generally would have satisfied the Court that the school board's reason was not pretextual.

When termination letters are used, there are risks if their contents are made public by either public or private employers. In *Oakes v. City of Fairhope*, the library director challenged, among other things, the contents of a letter from the library board terminating her employment.[20] The letter offered the librarian the opportunity to resign and explained why her employment was not to be continued. The letter was not kept in her personnel file nor was it shown to any prospective employer or otherwise made public. The Court denied her claim that the letter was defamatory or deprived her of a liberty interest, since the letter was not stigmatizing, not made public by the Board, was made in good faith, and was within the qualified privilege of fair comment on a public figure. The letter cited (1) a "fundamental philosophical difference" between the librarian and the Board as to the proper functions and division of authority between the director and the Board; (2) a belief that she did not have a proper rapport with the public; and (3) that a qualified person at a lesser salary could be found to do her job.[21]

EMPLOYMENT CRITERIA

If the lesson of the above cases is the proper use of personnel files and termination letters, other cases illustrate the need to articulate and fairly apply employment criteria such as academic credentials and experience. In *Gee*, the Library of Congress tried to establish that the plaintiff was not qualified for the position, which was posted as requiring an MLS degree with one year of experience or a bachelor's degree with three years of cataloguing or pertinent research experience at the GS-9 level. Ms. Gee had college courses but no degree; however, she had thirteen years of experience. Neither of the persons who held the job immediately prior to her application had any more college work than she. The Court ruled on her behalf, on the basis of her experience and the testimony of co-workers and others in personnel, that she was minimally qualified and that her race was a determining factor in the decision.

The substitution of experience for academic credentials, and *vice versa*, is an extremely troublesome area, and even the most precise description of actual skills required to perform a specific job will not avoid some nuisance suits in this area. A Chinese male PhD with no formal library education except four courses in bibliography applied for the position of Assistant Chief of the Orientalia Division at the Library of Congress. The recommending officer, who was of Japanese ancestry, selected another person for the job. The plaintiff alleged that he was discriminated against based on his national origin, citing what he termed longstanding enmity between the Chinese and Japanese.[22] Similarly, a Ukrainian male filed a national origin discrimination claim against the Library of Congress after being denied several positions for which he had applied, all of which required languages or background he didn't have. Any sympathy the court might have had was diluted by the evidence that the man had applied for LC positions three times a year for more than 10 years.[23]

The ALA-accredited MLS degree as a screening device must be used carefully. The burden is on the library to show that the degree is a valid criterion relative to the particular skills required for the specified job.

A case of some controversy in the library community which was decided in 1985, seems to endorse the use of the ALA-MLS as a screening device and may give libraries using it a false sense of security. In *Merwine v. Board of Trustees for State Institutions of Higher Learning*,[24] Glenda Merwine alleged intentional sex discrimination by Mississippi State University under Title VII and also alleged that the use of the published entry level requirement for a faculty librarian position—an MLS from a school accredited by the American Library Association—had an adverse impact on women in violation of Title VII.

Ms. Merwine's disparate treatment claims against defendant George Lewis, Library Director, were tried to a jury. The jury found that Ms. Merwine was qualified for the position but that preferential or favored treatment had been given to the successful male applicant, in that he was not qualified for the position and was nevertheless hired. Lewis filed a post-verdict motion, and the Magistrate set the verdict aside, concluding that no reasonable jury could have found for Ms. Merwine on the evidence produced with respect to her intentional discrimination, disparate treatment claims.

Ms. Merwine's disparate impact claims were tried to the Magistrate, who concluded that, in view of the fact that 80% of the ALA-MLS degrees awarded over the last 10-12 years have gone to women:

> [I]t flies in the face of logic and common sense to say that an ALA-MLS requirement 'selects applicants for hire' in a manner discriminatory to women.[25]

Thus, the Magistrate found that Ms. Merwine had failed to carry her burden of proving that the ALA-MLS degree requirement had a disproportionate or disparate impact on female applicants.

Because it found no disparate impact, The District Court never reached the issue of the validity of the ALA-MLS as a screening device either generally or for the specific vacancy at issue. Thus, that issue was not properly before the Court of Appeals. Nonetheless, in affirming the District Court's denial of Merwine's claims, the appeals court said:

> The uncontradicted evidence establishes that the ALA-MLS degree is a legitimate nondiscriminatory standard for hiring academic librarians. It is a standard widely recognized and utilized by academic and professional employers, including the United States Supreme Court.***
> . . . we believe the magistrate's holding that Merwine failed to establish her disparate impact claim *impliedly* included the finding that the ALA-MLS degree had a manifest relationship to the employment position at issue here.***
> Accordingly, sufficient evidence supports the magistrate's determination that a manifest relationship exists between the degree requirement and the position of librarian of the College of Veterinary Medicine at MSU.***
> . . . we believe that MSU's preference for an objective degree requirement that is widely recognized by academic and professional employers and that is required by approximately eighty percent of college and university libraries is supported as a valid business necessity.[26]

While the case has been heralded as a victory for proponents of the ALA-

MLS, it should be cautioned that despite its broad language, the case is limited in precedential value to the narrow issue of whether the ALA-MLS was a valid criterion for a single position at MSU.

Therefore, it is still true that the indiscriminate use of the ALA-MLS (or for that matter other educational credentials) as a selection device in hiring employees may run afoul of federal, state and local laws and regulations. If the use of a facially-neutral test has a disproportionate or disparate impact on a racial, ethnic or gender group, the employer must be able to establish that the use of such a device is a business necessity—that it validly predicts or is related to success on the job.[27]

The Equal Employment Opportunity Commission (EEOC) and other federal agencies involved in the enforcement of employment discrimination statutes developed the Uniform Guidelines on Employee Selection Procedures to provide guidance to employers on the permissible use of education requirements, tests and other facially neutral devices. They focus on two concepts: adverse impact and validation.

If use of a device results in a "substantially different rate of selection" to the disadvantage of a group, it may be said to have an "adverse impact" on that group.[28] The Uniform Guidelines specify that a selection rate for any protected group which is less than 4/5 of that for the highest group will generally be regarded as evidence of adverse impact. While this benchmark may not be appropriate in all cases, nonetheless it is a useful measure for an employer to use to determine whether selection devices have adverse impacts.

If a device does not have an adverse impact, there is no need to validate it. If the device does have an adverse impact, job-relatedness must be shown by professionally-accepted methods in a validity study. This involves an analysis of the job's tasks, skills and activities. Three means can be used: content validation, criterion validation and construct validation.

Briefly, content validation is established if the test closely approximates the actual tasks to be performed, e.g., a typing test for a typist's job.

If there is a significant correlation between the criteria and success on the job, criterion-related validation may be established.

Construct validation, which is rarely used, correlates the criterion and some trait (e.g., industry, intelligence, leadership) required on the job.

Since use of the ALA-MLS may pose some risk, and since a validity study may not be feasible for all libraries, library employers should take several steps to reduce their possible exposure and maximize the overall fairness of their selection procedures.

First, the library should analyze the positions to be filled to determine what the job actually entails and the kinds of skills, traits and experience realistically required to perform the job's tasks, in light of their relative importance. The library should review the background of employees who have successfully held those jobs in order to determine alternative qualification patterns that might suffice.

Second, the library should establish criteria for a job that are reasonably related to the actual work performed, e.g., an ALA-MLS is not a realistic requirement for a strictly clerical position.

Lastly, the library should be alert to detect whether its job criteria are having an adverse impact on any group and whether lesser criteria can be used with less adverse impact. The experience of other, comparable institutions may be useful in this last regard.

TERMINATION AND DISCIPLINE GENERALLY

Any termination or discipline of an employee is a fertile ground for suit, particularly if offending employees are not treated equally. The Library of Congress has been found not guilty of racial discrimination when it terminated black employees who had physical fights with their supervisors[29] or disrupted work with a demonstration during working hours on the premises,[30] and it successfully defended its decision not to promote an employee to sergeant in the Library's Special Police Force where the employee had problems with health, sobriety and absenteeism.[31] In such cases, the reasons for the employment decisions articulated by the library were found to be legitimate, and the treatment of the employees was not found to be different from the treatment of nonminorities in similar situations. Large libraries may have a history of disciplining employees that will help substantiate the nondiscriminatory nature of the library's action, but even smaller libraries should have standard procedures for dealing with such problems. The uniform application of such policies, of which all employees should be made aware, should help to avoid some lawsuits in this area.

EQUAL PAY

An illustrative case under the Equal Pay Act is *Lanegan-Gumm v. Library Association of Portland*,[32] decided in 1983. There a female bookmobile driver/clerk established that she was paid less for equal work than a male employee in the position of delivery truck driver. The Court required her to show that the two jobs involved:

1. equal skill,
2. equal effort,
3. equal responsibility, and
4. performance under similar conditions.

Substantial equivalence of the jobs, evaluated as a whole, is sufficient to trigger the requirements of the Act. In an Equal Pay action, the defendant may have an affirmative defense if he or she can prove that the wage differential is based on:

1. seniority system, or
2. a merit system, or
3. a system that measures earnings by quantity or quality, or
4. a differential based other than on sex.[33]

Whenever an Equal Pay action is brought, the plaintiff also has an opportunity to plead a violation of the Civil Rights Act as well, because even if the work is not substantially equal, it may be comparable enough to allow an inference that the different wage levels for the compared jobs results from intentional discrimination. In *Lanegan*, the Court found the two jobs substantially equal, even though the Library characterized one as clerical and one as physical. The Court also found disparate treatment in that historically the bookmobile driver always made less than the delivery truck driver.

One of the major issues in *Oakes* was a charge of sex discrimination. Although the terminated female librarian there was replaced by another female (at a lower salary), the plaintiff contended that there was an attitude of antagonism against her (hearsay sexual slurs, unidentified threatening phone calls, being followed by unidentified city trucks); that she was terminated not only because she was a woman but because she possessed traits and characteristics tolerable in a man but not in a woman, and that she was paid less than other city department heads who had less education. The court rejected the first two arguments for lack of evidence and held with respect to the third argument that a "meaningful comparison with regard to skill, effort and responsibility: was "virtually impossible."[34] Education alone, the court said, "simply does not address the nature of the duties in fact performed," and noted that municipalities were not required to fund non-essential city services on the same basis as "essential municipal services."[35]

Sex discrimination was the basis for an unsuccessful claim by a woman with an MLS degree who did not get a promotion in the Air Force to Chief of Acquisitions. In *Cavallari v. Stetson*,[36] the Air Force was able to show, using gender neutral criteria, that the male, who was not an MLS, was actually better qualified based on his additional six years of experience in the library. The Air Force argued that, as Chief of Acquisitions, the man had a broader-based view of the whole library than the female Chief of Cataloguing and was likely to be a better manager. Cavallari's record showed that her reports were weak and lacked detail and that she was single-minded in her view that the computer center was the most important concern facing the library.

By way of contrast, a Chinese woman successfully challenged the Library of Congress' failure to hire her as an Orientalia Division Section Head, despite her numerous qualifications, which included a BLS, a Master's in Asian History, and a PhD in Chinese History and command of four languages. The court held that she was entitled to an interview.[37]

Perhaps the more important issue now pending before the courts in the sex discrimination area is the issue of comparable worth–equal pay for work of equal value. The Equal Pay Act rejects the theory that employers should be obligated to give equal pay for comparable work where there is no substantial similarity in job content, so plaintiffs have turned to the somewhat broader provisions of Title VII, which specifically prohibits discrimination on account of sex. The gist of the complaint in these cases is that certain classes of jobs which are dominated by women pay less than jobs requiring comparable knowledge and skills, mental demands, accountability and working conditions.

The most significant victory for comparable worth proponents came in December, 1983, when a District Court in Washington State ruled that the State discriminated on the basis of sex against certain employees in particular classes of jobs by failing to adhere to the state's *own* study which evaluated the worth of these jobs.[38] While the case was settled while on appeal, it does portend increased litigation in this unresolved area of the law and indeed no less than 250 significant comparable worth cases are pending before the Equal Employment Opportunity Commission. Federal, state and municipal libraries and librarians will no doubt be markedly affected by future developments in this area.

REHABILITATION ACT OF 1973

The Rehabilitation Act of 1973 has also been enforced against at least one library. In *Hutchings v. Erie City and County, Inc.*,[39] a reference librarian charged discrimination in the following conduct by the defendant library:

1. forcing the librarian to work in a building which did not contain facilities for the handicapped;
2. demotion because of her handicap;
3. transfer to a job she was not physically capable of handling;
4. reprimands when the librarian protested working conditions;
5. refusal by the defendants to install handicapped facilities in the library until forced to do so by the threatened withdrawal of federal funding; and
6. harassment of the librarian when she filed administrative complaints protesting library policy.[40]

The court refused to summarily dismiss her claims, holding that the Act did create a private cause of action and that the plaintiff's remedies were not limited to simply monetary damages. The Act provides:

> No otherwise qualified handicapped individual in the United States . . . shall, solely by reason of his handicap be excluded from the participation in, be denied the benefits of, or be subjected to discrimination under any program or activity receiving federal financial assistance. . . .[41]

The final disposition of the case is not reported; however, the court did allow the possibility that the defendant library could show a good faith immunity defense as to some of the claims if it could show that the delay in remodeling the library was dictated by budgetary and administrative constraints and not by any animus directed towards the plaintiff. Such a defense, however, would only protect the defendant library from money damages, not from injunctive relief to stop the illegal action.

The Rehabilitation Act can also be used by plaintiffs who are not hired or promoted. In one kind of case, the defendant acknowledges that the handicap was a factor in reaching an employment decision and must argue that under all the circumstances there was a reasonable basis for concluding that a handicapped person was not qualified. In the second category, the defendant denies relying on the handicap in reaching an employment decision. In *Norcross v. Sneed*,[42] the plaintiff, who was legally blind, brought suit when she was not hired for the position of high school librarian. The court articulated how the Act is applied, stating that the plaintiff must show that he or she is an

> "otherwise qualified handicapped" individual, that she applied for the position as librarian and that she was rejected. If plaintiff satisfies this requirement, defendant must articulate legitimate, nondiscriminatory reasons for rejecting the plaintiff's application for the position. Having satisfied this requirement, the burden shifts to the plaintiff to show that the reasons offered are pretexted and that plaintiff was rejected solely because of her handicap. Plaintiff retains the ultimate burden of persuasion on the case as a whole to prove that she is an "otherwise qualified handicapped individual" and that she was rejected solely because of her handicap.[43]

There, the school board denied relying on the plaintiff's handicap and stated that she would have been hired but for the fact that the other candidate was more qualified. The court denied the plaintiff's claims. The case illustrates that in reaching hiring decisions concerning handicapped persons, it is important to be able to articulate a legitimate, nondiscriminatory reason for the choice that is made.

CONSTITUTIONAL RIGHTS

The First, Fifth, Ninth and Fourteenth Amendments can provide the basis for suits by terminated governmental employees charging abridgement of their privacy rights, freedom of speech and association or liberty interests and due process rights.

For instance, in *Hollenbaugh v. Carnegie Free Library*,[44] the fact that two library employees who were living together and having a child were terminated was held after careful consideration by the court not to violate any of those four amendments. There, a pregnant children's librarian, living with the married library janitor, protested their termination. The court held that the equal protection clause was not violated because the library did not have a policy of terminating such employees but rather had considered the effect the individuals' conduct would have on the library's ability "to properly perform its function in the community."[45] The court found it significant that the community was relatively small and that the employees had direct and frequent contact with the public. Thus, the court held that the termination of the employees was not arbitrary, capricious or unreasonable. Similarly, it held there was no fundamental right of privacy involved in discharging the employees under the peculiar circumstances of the case.

Free speech and liberty interests were also raised by a non-tenured university librarian whose employment was not renewed. The court in *Montgomery v. Boshears*,[46] reiterated that a non-tenured university employee has no property interest in continued employment which would require the procedural safeguards of due process. Similarly, the mere non-renewal of her employment did not stigmatize her in a way which violated her liberty interests, since the reasons for her non-renewal were not made public.

However, the court did examine the plaintiff's First Amendment claim, saying that even a non-tenured public employee cannot be denied renewal or account of the exercise of the employee's First Amendment rights. The plaintiff had criticized verbally and in writing the appointment of her supervisor and the implementation of the library computer system. Assuming these to be statements on matters of public concern, the court nonetheless denied the claim, holding that she failed to produce evidence that those expressions were a substantial or motivating cause for non-renewal in light of the university's evidence that she was not renewed primarily due to her insubordination and disruption of her department, independent of her criticism of the library.

CONCLUSION

The fact that libraries have not been a significant target for various types of employment litigation should not give rise to a false sense of security. Even one lawsuit, justified or not, can have a devastating effect on strained budgets as well as morale. Hopefully, libraries will continue to be sensitive to the complex legal environment in which they make employment decisions.

It is imperative that directors of libraries–both small and large, private and public–stay current as employment law develops and responds to new issues and new subtleties. At each library, at least one person should be trained to spot the issues raised at each step in the employment process and relationship–from developing job criteria to interviewing, selecting, evaluating, disciplining, paying, promoting and terminating an employee. As the case law makes clear, innocent motives will not protect employment practices which impose disparate treatment on employees. Self-assessment, education and indeed consultation with a lawyer are called for to insure that in the future, all persons have an equal opportunity to drive a bookmobile as well as enter the important profession of librarianship.

NOTES

1. *Brown v. Louisiana*, 383 U.S. 131, 137 (1966).
2. *Id.* at 142.
3. An initial search in the Labor Library, Cases File on Lexis on October 13, 1983 yielded 673 cases in which the word "Library" appeared; "Library w/10 defendant" yielded 58. A separate search for "Library w/50 defendant! but not prison but not correctional and date [after] 1/1/50" yielded 114. Of these, 28 actually involved libraries or library positions and were decided after 1965. An updated search on January 31, 1986 found 18 more cases, 7 of which pertained to cases involving libraries, although some were decided on purely procedural grounds. Additional cases no doubt have been brought and settled prior to adjudication; the search is not designed to be exhaustive.
4. 42 U.S.C. § 2000e-2.
5. 29 U.S.C. § 206(d)(l).
6. The Rehabilitation Act of 1973, 29 U.S.C. § 794 prohibits discrimination against the handicapped under any programs or activities receiving Federal financial assistance.
7. The Age Discrimination Act of 1975, 42 U.S.C. § 6102 prohibits unreasonable discrimination on the basis of age in programs or activities receiving Federal financial assistance, including revenue sharing funds.
8. 29 U.S.C. § 621.
9. 42 U.S.C. § 2000e-2.
10. *Jackson v. City of Killeen*, 654 F.2d 1181 (5th Cir. 1981).
11. *Id.*
12. *Id.* at 1183.
13. *Id.* at 1186.
14. *Gee v. Boorstin*, 500 F. Supp. 1025 (D.D.C. 1980).
15. *Lodico v. U.S.*, Civ. Action No. 77-72265 (S.D. Mich. Slip Opinion, December 3, 1982).
16. *Mandhare v. W.S. La Fargue Elementary School*, 605 F. Supp. 238 (E.D. La. 1985).
17. *Id.* at 239.
18. *Id.* at 240.
19. *Id.* at 241.

20. *Oakes v. City of Fairhope*, 515 F. Supp. 1004 (S.D. Ala. 1981).
21. *Id.* at 1015.
22. *Marynowych v. Boorstin*, 25 FEP Cases 1091 (D.D.C. 1977) *See also, Teemant v. Boorstin*, 23 FEP Cases 30, 9671 (D.D.C. 1980) [charge of discrimination in denial of employment due to Estonian nationality].
23. *Li v. Boorstin*, 17 FEP 8487 (D.D.C. 1978).
24. *Merwine v. Board of Trustees for State Institutions of Higher Learning*, 754 F.2d 631 (5th Cir. 1985).
25. *Merwine v. Board of Trustees for State Institutions of Higher Learning*, No. EC 81-154-WK-P (Memorandum Decision, N.D. Miss., December 29, 1983).
26. 754 F.2d at 638-640.
27. *Griggs v. Duke Power Co.*, 401 U.S. 424 (1971).
28. *See, Regner v. City of Chicago*, No. 83 C 6957 (Slip. Op. N.D. Ill. 1985) [discussion of use of statistics in unsuccessful case against Chicago Public Library by Filipino librarian denied promotion].
29. *Sullivan v. Boorstin*, 484 F. Supp. 836 (D.D.C. 1980).
30. *Bullock v. Boorstin*, 509 F.2d 384 (D.C. Cir. 1975).
31. *Garner v. Boorstin*, 29 FEP 1762 (D.D.C. 1981).
32. *Lanegan-Gumm v. Library Association of Portland*, 560 F. Supp. 486 (D. Ore. 1983).
33. 29 U.S.C. § 206.
34. *Oakes, supra* at n.14 at 1019.
35. *Id.* at 1019 fn.9.
36. *Cavallari v. Stetson*, 555 F. Supp. 561 (D. Mass. 1982).
37. *Wiens v. Boorstin*, 19 FEP Cases 186 (D.D.C. 1979).
38. *American Federation of State, County and Municipal Employees v. Washington*, No. C82-465T (1983).
39. *Hutchings v. Erie City and County, Inc.*, 516 F. Supp. 1265 (W.D. Pa. 1981) [no relation to the author].
40. *Id.* at 1266-67.
41. 42 U.S.C. § 794.
42. *Norcross v. Sneed* 755 F.2d 113 (8th Cir. 1985).
43. *Id.* at 116 fn.3.
44. *Hollenbaugh v. Carnegie Free Library*, 436 F. Supp. 1328 (W.D. Pa. 1977).
45. *Id.* at 1333.
46. *Montgomery v. Boshears*, 698 F.2d 739 (5th Cir. 1983).

Collective Bargaining and the Library Manager

Gwendolyn S. Cruzat

INTRODUCTION

In 1980, after considerable deliberation by the Ad Hoc Committee on Collective Bargaining of the American Library Association (ALA), the Council of ALA adopted as policy the following statement:

> The American Library Association recognizes the principle of collective bargaining as one of the methods of conducting labor-management relations used by private and public institutions. The Association affirms the right of eligible library employees to organize and bargain collectively with their employers, or to refrain from organizing and bargaining collectively, without fear of reprisal.[1]

Since ALA policy statements are by nature concise as possible, the members of the committee felt that the above statement did not reflect the total input of the members of the ALA and the effort made by the committee in responding to them. The committee held a number of hearings on the subject and invited representatives of all the type-of-library divisions, as well as any of the general membership who had an interest in the topic. One of the results of the hearings was that they made clear a major problem. The ALA membership is comprised of individuals, libraries/information units and other organizations interested in the library/information profession. This meant that the ALA included both employees and employers, public and private, including those who are not in library/information organizations.

In an effort to recognize all of these groups, the committee felt that it could not recommend any one model of collective bargaining or become a collective bargaining agent for the library/information profession. It did feel, however, that the ALA did have responsibility for educating and

---

Gwendolyn S. Cruzat, PhD (Wayne State), is a Professor at the School of Library Science, The University of Michigan, where she teaches among others a seminar on Collective Bargaining in Libraries. She served, in 1978-1980, as a chairperson of ALA Ad Hoc Committee on Collective Bargaining.

providing information to those groups or individuals that needed or requested it. The committee asked that guidelines be added to the policy stating that the ALA would:

1. inform librarians, other library employees, library administrators, trustees, boards of education, and appropriate officials about collective bargaining trends, methods, and techniques.
2. assist librarians, other library employees, library administrators, trustees, boards of education, union organizations, and appropriate officials in gathering data information to enable them to develop better employment patterns and contracts.
3. encourage and conduct educational programs to train librarians, other library employees, library administrators, trustees, boards of education, and appropriate officials in collective bargaining, and in working effectively within contractual employment patterns.
4. encourage type-of-library divisions to develop guidelines and recommendations for the pattern(s) of organization for collective bargaining for their type of institution.[2]

During the hearings, a number of views were presented. One of the most common was that the ALA was a professional organization and as such had responsibilities for promoting professionalism. Some members of ALA felt that by engaging in or even discussing collective bargaining in the context of the role that ALA might play was inappropriate. They adhered to standard definitions of "profession" and "professionalism" and felt that both indicated standards of excellence, proscribed ethics and responsibilities. They believed that librarianship is a profession and its members are bound by the standards of behavior that it has defined. They also felt the ALA, an association concerned with the professional interests of its membership, would compromise its status as a professional organization to that of a labor organization and be concerned only with strikes, wages and working conditions. In addition, these members equated collective bargaining with mediocrity and a decline in both the traditional merit reward system and in professionalism. On the other hand, there were those that felt that the ALA would be simply extending its interests to include wages and working conditions. This group of members believed that the attention given to these areas would improve significantly the profession's status and provide working conditions that would contribute to an increase in professionalism among the association's membership. The majority of the committee, while deliberating for a considerable length of time on the wording of its final statement, did not view the ALA as taking on the role of a union or collective bargaining agent due to the diverse composition of its membership.

One of the divisions that presented a strong and cogent statement to the committee was that of the library administrators. Earlier the division had constructed a statement with some of the components that appear in the "Guidelines" and they were of the opinion that just as employees had a right to bargain, they also had a right not to bargain. At the time this appeared to be a fairly conservative stance, even for library administrators; for during the 1970s collective bargaining had gained momentum, particularly among professionals, and appeared to be becoming a part of most environments, including those of libraries. Brooks and Odiorne state that during the 1970s everyone began to feel that to negotiate was a part of everyday life, a new, general-use tool of social relations.[3] The ALA policy, although passed at the beginning of the 1980s, more or less reflected the attitudes of the 1970s.

The 1980s, while echoing the attitudes of the 1970s, have introduced additional factors, an economic environment that has been affected by inflation, low economic growth and new advances in technology. Positions that became vacant through attrition were not being filled and the "new technology" has had a decided effect on employee reaction or participation in the work environment. The way these factors affect how employees of library/information or library related organizations will engage in collective bargaining is not clear. However, generally in environments where collective bargaining is present, there have appeared to be more compromises between employer and employee than were present during the 1970s. The 1980s, because of the manner in which the right to speak out and be heard in terms of decisions that affect one's life in general and one's work activity in particular, have begun to be seen as an era in which there may be changes in the way in which the negotiation/collective bargaining process is handled.

The principal purpose of this paper, then, is to relate some characteristics of the modern organization to contract or negotiated management and to identify some changes in approach that are relevant for library/information organizations management and may be relevant for the librarian/information professional for the rest of this decade and perhaps for the 1990s. The focus will be on the following areas: (1) characteristics of organizations, (2) contract or negotiated management, including enabling legislation and the nature of negotiating agents and (3) new issues and approaches for contract and negotiated management in the future. In the discussion that follows, statements made will have general applicability for all types of library/information environments. Notice will be made, however, regarding specific types of library/information units when possible.

CHARACTERISTICS OF ORGANIZATIONS

There often has been a reluctance to discuss organizational theory in an article of this nature, however, management experts have suggested that one of the reasons that organizations are surprised by their employees joining unions or engaging in collective bargaining is because the organizations have not subjected themselves to thorough analyses. While all libraries do not fall into this category, some do. Appropriate to any organization's analysis of itself is a theoretical framework of some kind. Katz and Kahn's typologies, based on the type of function or goal served by the organization appear to be applicable to library/information organizations. They describe five basic subsystems: (1) a production subsystem, concerned with the work that gets done, (2) a supportive subsystem, concerned with procurement, disposal and institutional relations, (3) maintenance, concerned with tying people into their functional roles and maintaining a stable environment, either through socialization or reward systems whether they be monetary, for prestige or for status, (4) adaptive, concerned with organizational change, sensing external changes and translating them for the good of the organization and (5) managerial, concerned with the direction and control of the many subsystems and activities of the structure, feedback or communication from units of the organization.[4] When analyses of organizations are attempted by managers or staff, they are based usually on the strengths or weaknesses of the very elements previously mentioned; that is whether the units are productive, whether the environment is stable, whether the organization adapts to change, either external or internal or whether there is communication or feedback, either vertical or horizontal. In other words, determinations are made as to effects of changes in the organization, e.g., as in its composition, in job requirements, in work attitudes, in work conditions, including new technology, in information or knowledge about the organization and in greater expectations in terms of the reward system.

Basically, when persons or human resources work together and share common experiences, they also tend to develop into subgroups and sometimes acquire goals of their own that may differ considerably from the goals of the organization. Although they may have shared values with the organization in which they work, there also may be conflicting values. These conflicting values may derive from such internal conflicts of interest with management as higher wages, the introduction of new technology which may appear as a job threat, the different interests of subgroups based on different positions and activities, better working conditions or simply the desire to be heard. In addition to internal factors, external factors that can influence the organization are the economy, the status of a profession and government regulations. Today, the greater the economic pressure, the less able the organization is to offer rewards, such as higher pay or tangible benefits. In some instances, if the employees are attempting to advance themselves and their professional status or have concerns about their professional development, the organization may be able to offer nonmonetary rewards, but if personal or group goals are not achieved, conflicts may result. Conversely, if the organization attempts to improve its status by requiring that new technologies be implemented, the employees may resist. Kochan and Verma further emphasize that some of the reasons that negotiations or collective bargaining arise in organizations is because of decision-making that involves more than one party who hold conflicting interests, as well as sufficient common interests, that cause each to remain within the relationship. This also involves some type of reciprocity.[5]

The above brief discussion of organizational characteristics and value conflicts may indicate why some library institutions or organizations embrace collective bargaining and why others do not. If these conflicts cannot be resolved through some of the more well known management methods, such as participatory management, management by objectives, strategic planning or some organizational structure that supports development or change strategies which stress interpersonal trust and open communication lines; then contract or negotiated management comes into play. The forms most recognized are (1) "meet and confer" negotiated management where neither side is legally bound but negotiation takes place, particularly on issues other than salaries or wages; and (2) collective bargaining which is legally binding.

COLLECTIVE BARGAINING LEGISLATION, UNITS AND AGENTS

One external factor previously mentioned that determines the degree to which collective bargaining can be used as a management tool is that of labor relations legislation and regulations. Collective bargaining is an interactive process in which unions or bargaining agents and private or public employers or management negotiate the rules that govern employment. The right to engage in collective bargaining in both the private and public sectors is granted by legislation. In the private sector, concern is primarily with one Federal statute, the National Labor Relations Act of 1935 (Wagner Act), as amended by the Labor Management Relations Act of 1947 (Taft-Hartley Act) and the Labor Management Reporting and Disclosure Act of 1959 (Landrum-Griffin Act). Under this legal framework, the National Labor Relations Board (NLRB), the implementing unit makes decisions and issues orders on collective bargaining for both employers and unions.[6] Administrative law, in the form of President Kennedy's Executive Order 10988 and President Nixon's Executive Order 11491 provided a basis for collective bargaining among local, state and Federal agency employees by giving Federal employees the right to join or not join unions.[7]

Other legislation that has affected collective bargaining is (1) the Equal Pay Act of 1963 that prohibits employers from discriminating on the basis of sex in payment of wages; (2) the Civil Rights Act of 1964, as amended by the Equal Employment Opportunity Act of 1972, that prohibits discrimination in employment on the basis of race, color, sex, religion or natural origin and covers both private and public employers with fifteen or more employees, private and public educational institutions, except for religious institutions, and state and local governments; (3) the Age Discrimination Act of 1967, as amended in 1978, that prohibits discrimination based on age; (4) the Occupational and Safety Act of Act of 1970 that ensures commercial employers provide safe and healthy working conditions; and (5) the Civil Service Reform Act of 1978, that provided for Federal employees, other than postal employees, the right to belong to unions and bargain collectively.[8]

However, with the passage of the Taft-Hartley Act in 1947, collective bargaining became available to professional employees, but the NLRB in a 1951 decision regarding Columbia University refused to include in its jurisdiction those nonprofit, educational institutions it considered to be involved also in charitable and educational activities of a nonacademic nature. However, in what is termed a landmark case, the NLRB in 1970 reversed its earlier decision when it ruled in case of Cornell University that nonprofit, private, educational institutions could be required to bargain with their employees. At that time the NLRB admitted that it was entering an uncharted area and would proceed on a case by case basis. The NLRB asserted that the principles used in the industrial area were reliable guides to organizations in the educational context. The Cornell case involved only nonacademic employees, but the NLRB took jurisdiction over academic employees when it established a broad unit, including faculty, counselors, librarians and other support staff in a decision on the C.W. Post Center, Long Island University. In this decision department chairmen were excluded from the unit as supervisors. In a later decision involving academic employees at Fordham University, the NLRB decided that while faculty could recommend policy to the university, no faculty member had decision-making authority. It further assumed that faculty were not supervisors because of their relationship to their graduate assistants, which is a teacher-student rather than an employer-employee relationship. At Yeshiva University the NLRB found faculty to be managers and therefore decided that they could not bargain.[9]

Both the Cornell decision, as well as subsequent decisions, and the interpretation made by the NLRB regarding application of industrial area collective bargaining guidelines to academic institutions seem to indicate that the NLRB views academic environments as more than collegial communities. Today, more than when the decisions were made, this should come as no surprise, for the academic institution itself has changed. It is viewed more as a business enterprise with a product, its graduates. The determination that faculty have no decision-making powers should be of particular import to those directors or managers who believe that libraries/information centers should become more like the college or university departments and librarians/information specialists should take on some of the roles of faculty. It should also be of interest to those institutions where faculty status for librarians is of major importance. There is no doubt that faculty power has eroded to a great extent and those opponents of faculty status for librarians may be correct when they state that members of the library/information profession in academic environments should not emulate the faculty.

Definitions that are fundamental to the National Labor Relations Act (NLRA) and to the NLRB decisions are distinctly industrial or bureaucratic in nature. The NLRA defines a supervisor as:

> any individual having authority, in the interest of the employer, to hire, transfer, suspend, lay off, recall, promote, discharge, assign, reward, or discipline other employees, or responsibility to direct them, or to adjust their grievances, or effectively recommend such action, if in connection with the foregoing the exercise of such authority is not in a merely routine or clerical nature, but requires the use of independent judgment.[10]

Its definition of a professional is:

> any employee engaged in work (i) predominantly intellectual and varied in character as opposed to routine mental, manual, mechanical, or physical work; (ii) involving the consistent exercise of discretion and judgment in its performance; (iii) of such a character that the output produced or the result accomplished cannot be standardized in relation to a given period of time; (iv) requiring knowledge of an advanced type in a field of science or learning customarily acquired by a prolonged course of specialized instruction and study in an institution of higher learning or hospital, as distinguished from a general academic education or from an apprenticeship or from training in the performance of routine, mental, manual, or physical processes; or any employee who (i) has completed the courses of specialized intellectual instruction and study described in clause (iv) . . . and (ii) is performing related work under the supervision of a professional person to qualify himself to become a professional employee as defined.[11]

While supervisors are excluded from the definition of employee and consequently not covered by the NLRA, interpretation is based on whether or not they have real authority over employees rather than a title that appears to give authority. Similarly, professionals can be challenged or excluded if they do not appear to meet all of the requirements as defined. Some librarians or information specialists may find themselves designated as employees, rather than supervisors, or nonprofessionals, rather than professionals.[12] This decision was made in a governmental unit, which means that it could apply to four-year or community colleges, school systems and public libraries that are legally tied to school systems.

Although the specific definitions stated previously emanate from Federal legislation, in states where collective bargaining legislation has been enacted, these definitions usually have been adopted by the state government agencies. The adoption of Federal agency definitions is common practice in states with collective bargaining legislation because few attempts have been made to establish uniform law or to propose a model law. Consequently, states and municipalities vary in the comprehensiveness of the legislation. Collective bargaining in the public sector does not have the clear-cut authority that is present for the private sector. Public academic institutions, school districts and public libraries are able to bargain only if the state provides coverage. For example, in Texas the statute mandates (under community option) collective bargaining for police and firefighters only. Usually the coverage is more restrictive than that provided by Federal legislation and there is no guarantee that interpretation will be the same for the public institution as it is for the private.

In addition, the NLRA forbids the placing of professional employees in a bargaining unit with nonprofessional workers unless a majority of professionals vote for it. However, both Federal and state collective bargaining legislation identifies bargaining unit determination as the first step in the collective bargaining process, whether by mutual consent of those seeking recognition as a unit or by Federal or state labor agency decision. Unit determination is one of the most significant steps because, in addition to establishing the persons who are represented, it has a decided impact upon the negotiations.

In academic institutions membership has been determined usually case by case, based primarily on a combination of conditions or attitudes at the institution. In the earlier years of bargaining at academic institutions, librarians were welcomed into the bargaining unit. One of the reasons was that it increased the power of those forming the unit and the agent representing the unit. In these instances librarians believed they would achieve some type of parity with faculty in terms of both wages and status. In school districts librarians generally have been included with teachers and have appeared to receive to a greater degree than the academic librarians more equitable treatment. However, Billings states that media/library professionals who teach in the K-12 area are a minority of the larger K-12 teachers unit.[13] Other problems may occur in that treatment in the unit is dependent upon location and whether the employer is the school board, the city council or the state. In public libraries, where there are multi-tiered units, both management and librarians have had more control over their own destinies than either of the other groups because generally the only environment considered in bargaining is that of the library. Library managers in all of these environments may find themselves carrying out rules or conditions of employment that do not easily fit into the library environment. Public libraries are least likely to be in this situation, but they too may be a part of bargaining units for city or state government agencies. In addition, library directors or managers may also find themselves in a unit with persons with whom they have little or nothing in common. Library managers in the public sector also have to deal with political and legislative realities.

The union or collective bargaining agent with whom management has to deal has been described as having an impact on the atmosphere in which bargaining takes place, particularly since collective bargaining is considered to be an adversarial relationship between employer and employees. There are a number of national unions that are involved with library/information professionals. They are the American Association of University Professors (AAUP), the National Education Association (NEA), the American Federation of Teachers (AFT) and the American Federation of State, County, and Municipal Employees (AFSME), as well as the United Auto Workers (UAW) and the Teamsters' Union. In addition, there are numerous local unions with no national affiliations.

There may be variations in approaches used by these unions or agents or some may be considered more militant than others, but they are all bargaining over the distribution of power in the organization. Management's responsibility in this area is to secure as much information regarding the union or collective bargaining agent and the type of methods that they use. This includes determining or securing the type of contract they generally negotiate.

MANAGEMENT AND THE COLLECTIVE BARGAINING PROCESS

The collective bargaining process, sometimes referred to as collective bargaining by objectives in the 1980s, has retained basically its negotiation characteristics. Primary components of the process for management are: (1) review of any previous negotiations, (2) review of the previous contract, (3) the bargaining agent, (4) internal and external information, (5) bargaining strategies, (6) collective bargaining agent or union demands, and (7) possibility of a strike.[14]

1. Review of any previous negotiations—Management must review any negotiations made during the previous year, even if it is a first

effort to bargain collectively. All problems, successes or failures, individually or collectively, should be reviewed. Persons key to past interactions should be identified and their role in current negotiations should be clarified. If it is not a first contract, then all negotiations or agreements should be reviewed to determine if there are still problems or if the bargaining objectives have been met. In addition, persons who had influence in past negotiations should be identified and their roles reviewed for current negotiations. One of the failures of managers in the bargaining process is to use their middle managers and supervisors to point out key problems in day to day operations. In academic and school libraries this information usually is provided to the chief executive officer (CEO) or his or her designated representative. In the public library the director of the library may be the CEO.

2. Review of the last contract—Management must review the last contract to determine if there are any areas that need clarification or modification. This is where middle managers or supervisors can play a significant role. They can aid in the identification of grievances filed or problems areas that are not covered sufficiently by the present contract. Management may wish to make some effort to see that some of these problems are resolved before negotiations begin. If this is not possible, plans may be developed to handle these problems.
3. The bargaining unit—If this is a new contract, management should examine the makeup of the unit and its cohesiveness. If it is not a new contract, management should determine if there has been any attempt during the term of the contract for groups to be added or if there has been any change in the cohesiveness of the unit. In public libraries particularly, there should be an evaluation of the relationships of units with whom they bargain if there is more than one contract with the same agent.
4. Internal and external information—Collection and thorough analysis of information regarding wages and benefits is one of the most important features of the negotiation process. This includes information on departments, job classification, salaries or wage rates, hours of work, overtime work, number of employees and age and years of service, health and life insurance costs and any other items that might be useful during negotiations. Also included should be the provisions that are in the current contract and any problems that have occurred regarding them. External information that is of importance relates to legislation that is applicable to the workplace and changes in that legislation. National and state legislation, as well as NLRB and court decisions, have had an impact on rules and regulations in the workplace. Other external information that is useful is that of a general nature, e.g., rate of inflation, rate of unemploy-

ment, salary or wage figures in comparable environments, collective bargaining contracts for similar units in other environments and communication with other library directors or managers in similar environments. In addition, management should secure a list of the collective bargaining agent's officers, its financial report and its publications. In some environments, a labor relations office is responsible for the collection of some of this information, but the library managers are responsible for provision of information about their departments to the labor relations officer or CEO.

5. Management's strategies – Management should set its own agenda and establish its own objectives for bargaining. It should determine from the above information what changes it wishes to make in terms of economic or noneconomic provisions. Rationales and data should be prepared to support management's position. Summations regarding proposals and counterproposals should be prepared. Timetables and guidelines should be established for management to follow during the bargaining process. Although library directors or managers may not be representatives at the bargaining table, progress is communicated to them and additional information may be expected from them at some time during bargaining. Usually, methodology for communication is predetermined. Management selects its spokesperson and team and determines the team's authority, including information that may be given to the general public. In some instances the CEO has stated what management proposes prior to bargaining. In addition, management comes to some agreement with the union as to where bargaining will take place and what support services will be needed. One of the problems in the academic environment and in some instances in other environments has been the fact that professors or librarians have felt that they can negotiate for the profession better than an outsider, e.g., national agents or unions, lawyers, and consequently have been at a disadvantage at the bargaining table. This is also true of management in some environments where they have failed to secure the expertise of those familiar with the bargaining arena. However, the professional negotiator must be familiar with the environment, otherwise he or she may produce the same results as the inexperienced negotiator.
6. Collective bargaining units or union demands – The demands of the collective bargaining unit should have been anticipated by previous research done by management. When received it should be analyzed and cost estimates made for each demand. Management may then determine the stand it will make on each demand and prepare its statements or arguments or its own solutions.
7. Possibility of a strike – Management should always anticipate that a strike may occur and make plans to deal with that possibility. There are many additional suggestions that have been made regarding the

process such as maintaining a positive attitude, being assertive and having good coping abilities. Suggestions have been made that there should be an attempt to select a negotiating team comparable in age, sex and racial composition to that of the union. The collective bargaining or negotiation process, described here briefly, is generally considered to be an adversarial process. However, during this decade the terms concession and collaborative bargaining have appeared and while the steps in the bargaining process basically are the same, there are differences that are beneficial to management.

COLLECTIVE BARGAINING IN THE 1990S

Collective bargaining for the rest of this decade and in the 1990s for those in the library/information profession will be either quite adversarial or will be what has been termed concession or collaborative bargaining. There are two major factors that will determine the outcome. First, the library/information professional is a white-collar employee, better educated and better informed. This professional wants to be treated as an equal. Freeman has stated that if the types of persons with whom management deals approve of antiunion behavior or at least don't disapprove, then it's much easier for management.[15] The library/information profession, concerned with its status and professionalism tends to fall within Freeman's description. In addition, the library/information profession is a part of the larger information technological workforce. Peitchinis has stated that considering the changes that continue to take place in technology and the rate of that change, human adjustments to such changes will become central issues in union-management relations.[16] Coupled with the economic pressures of the times, a different set of circumstances comes into play. The second factor is that managers of today's libraries or information centers or the CEOs of the parent institutions are a new breed of managers for the most part. They have been taught to manage by objectives or to use participatory management or to plan strategically. They have been urged to involve all the members of their departments, or schools or libraries to become active in committees or task forces or working groups to solve the problems of the library/information environments. They have been successful in seeking out problem areas and using the professional staff to solve them, specifically including those of salaries and rewards in the workplace. They have devised professional development programs and sophisticated grievance procedures in their environments. The Association of Research Libraries (ARL) has been adept at providing its membership with assistance that has aided in the management of libraries, for example, a kit on collective bargaining.[17] Management may not have been successful always in their endeavors, but the professionals and other workers in the environment have felt that efforts have been made on their behalf. They have diffused the adversarial environment that is a part of collective bargaining by offering a more attractive work environment. In other words, today's managers are in the driver's seat. They have made management rights as important as union rights by creating a different environment. In addition, many of the rules and regulations of the workplace have been made through legislative fiat. The manager today can point to a regulation that makes it possible or impossible for him or her to take action regarding some grievances.

As a consequence of the factors mentioned above and the economic environment, many unions or bargaining agents have found themselves in the position of concession bargaining. They have been willing to bargain away wages and benefits for job security. They have agreed to waive or suspend future economic benefits for a period of time.[18] They have also been willing to negotiate for nonmonetary items, such as how grievances are handled. Concession bargaining started with industry during the economic recess, has continued in the late 1980s and probably will continue to play a major role in the 1990s. In the library/information environment this may be inevitable because of the increased role technology will play. CEOs of some major health centers have indicated that libraries will exist in the centers, but they may be places that no one frequents.[19]

They foresee for the future computer access to libraries in such a manner that will cause a reconfiguration, even more so than today, regarding how professionals are used. The result will be that there may be fewer positions for library/information professionals or that they may be used in very different ways from present position descriptions or classifications. Saving positions or job security is very important to white-collar workers. They are not as willing as the blue-collar workers to strike, especially if they are in public institutions where strikes are usually illegal. A recent example of concession bargaining took place in Michigan, known as a state favorable toward collective bargaining. Faculty at Wayne County Community conceded an increase in wages for a no layoff clause.[20] However, if and when there is a change for the better in the economic climate and professionals determine that their concessions have not been returned, the adversarial bargaining process may return.

Cross, among others, asks whether our traditional collective bargaining processes and procedures are effectively applicable today.[21] Suggestions have been made that a better way of bargaining in the future is that of collaborative bargaining. It is in the mold of flexible management and may be more broadbased than the present process. The involvement of professionals through professional development, team building and consensus decision-making may result in managers and professionals sharing information and knowledge.[22] Better interpersonal relationships and communications are the keys. One of the criteria, however, is that both management and employees feel that the outcome will be beneficial for both. In any event, the impact of technology, the growing ranks of the service industry and continued low economic growth will cause additional changes and problems in libraries and information centers that may be aided by a different type of bargaining. Although concession bargaining is present and may continue for some time to come, it will not be permanent. There has been growth, however, in alternatives to the bargaining process with today's managers in exchange for providing increases in salaries, providing professionals with increases in decision-making or job security. These kinds of alternatives may cause the roles of unions to be changed. Library/information managers in the 1990s can, for the option will be theirs, determine whether or not the collective bargaining process will be an adversarial or collaborative process.

NOTES

1. *American Library Association Policy Manual*. Policy No. 54.11.
2. Ibid.
3. Earl Brooks and George S. Odiorne. *Managing by Negotiations*. New York: Van Nostrand Reinhold, 1984.
4. Daniel Katz and Robert L. Kahn. *The Psychology of Social Organizations*. 2d. ed. New York: John Wiley, 1978, p. 84. Although Katz and Kahn's theory is used as the theory for this discussion, other organizational theories may be appropriate and preferred.
5. Thomas A. Kochan and Anil Verma. "Negotiations in Organizations: Blending Industrial Relations and Organizational Behavior Approaches," in *Negotiating in Organizations* by Max H. Bazerman and Roy J. Lewicki, eds. Beverly Hills: Sage, 1983, p. 14.
6. National Labor Relations Act (Wagner Act). Statutes at Large 49, sec. 372, 449 (1935). U.S. Code, vol. 29, sec. 151-169 (1982); Labor Management Relations Act (Taft-Hartley Act), Statutes at Large 61, sec. 120, 136 (1947), U.S. Code, vol. 29, sec. 151-169 (1982); Labor-Management Reporting and Disclosure Act (Landrum-Griffin Act), Statutes at Large 49, sec. 301, 519 (1959), U.S. Code, vol. 29, sec. 151-169 (1982).
7. U.S. President. Executive Order 10988. "Employee-Management Cooperation in the Federal Service." *Federal Register* 27, 17 January 1962, 551; U.S. President. Executive Order 11491. "Labor-Management Relations in the Federal Service." *Federal Register* 34, 29 October 1969, 17605.
8. Equal Pay Act, vol. 42, sec. 206; Civil Rights Act, vol. 42, sec. 1971 ff; Age Discrimination Act, vol. 29, sec. 621-634; Equal Employment Opportunity Act, vol. 42, sec. 1971 ff; Occupational Health and Safety Act, vol. 29, sec. 553, 651-678; Employment Equity Act, vol. 42, sec. 206; Civil Service Reform Act, vol. 5, sec. 1101; U.S. Code (1982).
9. Columbia University, 97 NLRB No. 72, 29 Labor Relations Reference Manual 1098 (1951); Cornell University, 183 NLRB No. 141, 74 Labor Relations Reference Manual 1270 (1970); Fordham University, 193 NLRB No. 23, 78 Labor Relations Manual 1177 (11971); Long Island University (C.W. Post), 189 NLRB No. 109, 77 Labor Relations Reference Manual 1001 (1972).
10. National Labor Relations Act, sec. 151-169 (1982).
11. National Labor Relations Act, sec. 151-169 (1982).
12. U.S. Department of Labor, Decisions and Reports on Rulings of Assistant Secretary of Labor for Labor-Management Relations Pursuant to Executive Order 11491, vol. 2, January 1-December 31, 1972, A/SLMR No. 224.
13. Rolland G. Billings and Errol Goldman, *Professional Negotiations for Media/Library Professionals: District and School*. Washington, D.C.: Association for Educational Communications and Technology, 1980, p. 2.
14. Numerous authors have written regarding the collective bargaining or negotiating process

from the management perspective and the process has been basically the same with only minor differences in approach. These authors are listed in the bibliography for this paper. This process in this paper is adapted from those authors or editors who have written or collected papers on this subject, e.g., Dilts, Bazerman, Ewing, Rabin and Baderschneider.

15. Fortune Panel, "Are the Unions Dead or Just Sleeping?" *Fortune*, vol. 106, p. 101.

16. Stephen G. Peitchins, *Issues in Management-Labour Relations in the 1990s*. New York: St. Martin's Press, 1985, p. 136.

17. Association of Research Libraries, Office of Management Studies. *Unionization in ARL Libraries*. Kit 118. Washington, D.C.: ARL, 1985.

18. Leland B. Cross, "1982 and 1983: The Concession Bargaining Years: Economic Restructuring Will Recast Labor Relations," *Personnel Administrator*, November 1984, p. 27.

19. Association of Computer Resources in the Academic Health Center. *Executive Management*. Washington, D.C.: 1984, p. 17.

20. Karen Schneider, "Profs Swap Wages for Layoff Ban," *Detroit Free Press*, March 27, 1986, sec. A, p. 3.

21. Leland B. Cross, p. 35.

22. Thomas A. Kochan and Verma Anil, pp. 24-25.

REFERENCES

American Library Association Policy Manual. Policy No. 54.11.

Association of Computer Resources in the Academic Health Center. *Executive Management*. Washington, D.C.: 1984, p. 17.

Association of Research Libraries, Office of Personnel Management Studies. *Unionization in ARL Libraries*. Kit 118. Washington, D.C.: ARL, 1985.

Baderschneider, Jean A., ed. *The Collective Bargaining Process: Readings and Analysis*. Plano, Texas: Business Publications, 1983.

Barron, Daniel, ed. "The School Library Media Professional in the Negotiations Process," *School Media Quarterly*, Summer 1983, pp. 265-303.

Bazerman, Max H., ed. *Negotiating in Organizations*. Beverly Hills, CA: Sage, 1983.

Billings, Rolland G. *Professional Negotiations for Media/Library Professionals: District and School*. Washington, D.C.: Association for Educational Communications and Technology, 1980.

Birnbaum, Robert. *Creative Academic Bargaining*. New York: Columbia University, 1980.

Blevins, Ronald A. "Maximizing Company Rights Under the Contract: A Guide for Training First-Line Supervisors," *Personnel Administrator*, June 1984, pp. 75-82.

Brooks, Earl and Odiorne, George S. *Managing by Negotiations*. New York: Van Nostrand Reinhold, 1984.

Cross, Leland B. "1982 and 1983: The Concession Bargaining Years: Economic Restructuring Will Recast Labor Relations," *Personnel Administration*, November 1984, pp. 27-35.

Dilts, David A. and Deitsch, Clarence R. *Labor Relations*. New York: Macmillan, 1983.

Ewing, David. W. *Do It My Way or You're Fired: Employee Rights and the Changing Role Of Management Prerogatives*. New York: John Wiley, 1983.

Fischer, Russell. "Collective Bargaining for Librarians: An Interview with Philip Hoehn," *Wilson Library Bulletin*, December 1983, pp. 274-276.

Fortune Panel. "Are the Unions Dead or Just Sleeping?" *Fortune*, vol. 106, 101 ff.

Hoover, John J. "Union Organization Attempts: Management's Response," *Personnel Journal*, March 1982, pp. 214-219; "Negotiating the Initial Union Contract," *Personnel Journal*, September 1982, pp. 692-698.

Howard, Dennis R. "Factors Affecting the Attitudes of Public Managers Toward Collective Bargaining," *Journal of Collective Negotiations*, vol. 12, 1983, pp. 99-107.

Katz, Daniel and Kahn, Robert L. *Psychology of Organizations*. 2d ed. New York: John Wiley, 1978.

Lilore, Doreen. *The Local Union in Public Libraries*. Hamden, CN: Shoestring Press, 1984.

Michelson, David. W. "Labor Relations Update: Beware of GAPS in Collective Bargaining," *Personnel*, April 1985, pp. 73-76.

Munchus, George. "Collective Bargaining and the Future of the Federal Merit System of Human Resource Administration," *Journal of Collective Negotiations*, vol. 11, 1982, pp. 297-303.

Nigro, Lloyd. "Collective Bargaining and the Attitudes of Local Government Personnel Managers," *Public Personnel Management Journal*, vol. 9, 1980, pp. 160-171.

O'Reilly, Robert C. and O'Reilly, Margaret I. *Librarians Labor Relations Employment Under Union Contracts*. Westport, CN: Greenwood, 1981.

Peitchinis, Stephen G. *Issues in Management-Labour Relations in the 1990s*. New York: St. Martin's Press, 1985.

Rabin, Jack, ed. *Handbook on Personnel Administration and Labor Relations*. New York: Marcel Dekker, 1983.

Rosenthal, Mary. "The Impact of Unions on Salaries in Public Libraries," *Library Quarterly*, vol. 55, 1985, pp. 52-70.

Schneider, Karen. "Profs Swap Wages for Layoff Ban," *Detroit Free Press*, March 27, 1986, sec. A, p. 3.

Simpson, Paul. "Collective Bargaining: Management's Opportunity to Improve Labor Economics," *Employee Relations Law Journal*, vol. 11, Summer, 1985, pp. 72-88.

Todd, Katherine. "Collective Bargaining and Professional Associations in the Library Field," *Library Quarterly*, vol. 55, 1985, pp. 284-299.

Wall, James A. *Negotiation: Theory and Practice*. Glenview, IL: Scott, Foresman, 1985.

Wilson, Karen. "Federal Sector Labor-Management Relations: A Guide to Decisional Materials Relating to Title VII of the Civil Service Reform Act of 1978," in *Labor, Work-Life and Industrial Relations*. The Haworth Press, 1984, pp. 87-99.

Wooldridge, Ewart. "Negotiating Technology," *Personnel Management*, October 1982.

Zack, Arnold M. and Bloch, Richard. *Labor Agreement in Negotiation and Arbitration*. Washington, D.C.: Bureau of National Affairs, 1983.

Copyright: A Lasting Question for Managers

William Z. Nasri

LEGAL NATURE OF COPYRIGHT

The term "Copyright" has a double meaning stemming from its etymology. It denotes the right "to own and control a work of authorship" in addition to the right to "copy it." The English term, for historical reasons, does not, however, identify the beneficiary in the rights. Conversely, the said beneficiary is clearly identified in equivalent terms in other languages such as in French "Droit D'Auteur," in German "Urherberrecht" and in Spanish "Derecho del Autor." All mean "the right of the author."

Copyright is a part of what is known as intellectual property which includes also patent and trademarks. In general, copyright is a unique property right that rewards the authors for their contributions to society and entices them to contribute to the advancement of knowledge. The difference between these three different types of proprietary rights is that copyright protects only the independently created words and arrangements of an author in relation to any idea. Copyright does not extend its protection to the idea itself. Therefore, ideas are free and can be built upon and be expressed differently and the expression can be protected even if it discusses a subject that is already in existence and in fact protected. Patent, on the other hand, protects both the idea and its expression in any given invention, provided that the latter is novel, useful and nonobvious to an expert in the field. A patentee has a monopoly right (for 17 years in the U.S.) to prevent others from using his/her invention, in part or in toto, even if others made the same discovery independently. Trade-

---

William Z. Nasri, JD, PhD (Pittsburgh), is a professor at the School of Library and Information Science, University of Pittsburgh, and the Coordinator of the Management of the Library and Information Services' area in the Department of Library Science. He serves also as a Copyright Consultant to the same University and to several other institutions. He is a writer and a national speaker on the legal issues involved in library and information management and he lectures annually at the Library Administrators Development Program at the University of Maryland. He is PLA Liaison to ALA Ad Hoc Committee on Copyright and he has served for several years on the Advisory Board of the Copyright Clearance Center.

This article is reprinted with permission of the author. It is based on his article "Copyright" which appeared in ALA World Encyclopedia of Library and Information Services, 2nd edition, 1986.

marks protection is not based on creative authorship but on the investment and skill in soliciting a symbol which the public will readily identify with a particular goods or service.

There are two major schools of thought in relation to the legal nature of copyright. One school considers copyright as a type of alienable property such as real stock and goods. As such this school advocates unlimited, perpetual rights to the owner of copyright. The second school believes that copyright is a monopoly and since the latter, in any form, has bad economic and social implications, the author should be given as little protection as possible. Some Western European countries (e.g., France) recognize copyright as a unique form of property rights with strong personal elements at its base. These countries recognize this personal right in their laws and grant the author an inalienable "Moral Right" which assures his identification with the work and protects against its distortion or any alteration that might be prejudicial to the author's reputation or honor. This "personal" approach to copyright was the philosophy behind what is known today as the Berne Convention.

HISTORY AND PRESENT STATUS OF COPYRIGHT

The "copyright" concept started in 17th century England after the printing press was brought to England from Germany. When William Caxton brought the movable type printing press to England in 1476, the production of a book was revolutionized. As a result, any given work was easily produced in multiple copies. It created also a threat for the publisher of the works whose original work could be reproduced easily by "pirates" without bearing any of the cost involved in the production of the first copy of it. To protect themselves, the publishers, booksellers and printers created a trade association and called it the Stationers' Company, which was chartered later in 1557 by Queen Mary. In accordance with this Charter, the Stationers maintained a register in which the members recorded the title of each book they bought from an author or from another member. An entry in the said register granted the registrant perpetual rights in the registered book and later determined claims of piracy. A decade later, most regulations, including the Stationers' rules to control the press, were proven ineffective and nonenforceable. By 1710, the Statute of Anne was enacted as the first English copyright law. The Statute granted protection against unauthorized printing/copying of published works for a limited period of time. Unpublished works were covered by common law and not protected by the Statute of Anne. One might consider the said Statute to be the prototype of all subsequent copyright laws in the civilized world. For example, it was, in concept, the basis for article 1, section 8 of the U.S. Constitution which vested the congress with the power to create a law that gives the authors and inventors for a limited time, exclusive rights to their writings and discoveries, for the purpose of the "advancement of science and useful arts." In 1790, the first U.S. copyright law was enacted and applied only to books, maps and charts. Since it granted protection only to U.S. citizens, foreign authors such as Charles Dickens, were fully pirated by U.S. publishers to the exclusion of American authors. In 1891, the Chase Act passed the Congress granting protection to foreign authors, under certain conditions, thus protecting consequently American authors from the unfair competition with royalty free pirated English works.

The 1790 law was amended several times mainly to expand the subject matter protected by its provisions. For example, in 1802 the Congress extended copyright protection to prints, in 1831 the public performance became protected, and in 1870, fine arts in addition to the rights to dramatization and translation were included. A major revision took place in 1909 and it included still more categories of protective work (such as "plastic works of scientific or technical character"). The right of the author to make derivations (e.g., abridgments) from his/her original work was also added to the bundle of the author's rights. In 1947, the law was codified and enacted as Title 17 of the U.S. Code. In 1971, the sound recording was added as the seventh category of protective works of authorship. The period of protection under the 1909 law was 28 years renewable for a similar period. The dramatic changes in our society and the vast advancement in technology after World War II dictated the necessity to review the 1909 law to respond to such changes. In October 17, 1976, the Congress passed a general revision of the law which had a profound effect on the copyright system. The 1976 revision, which was enacted in 1978, preempted common law copyright (i.e., unpublished works are now protected for a period of 100 years from the date of creation and not in perpetuity). The period of protection for works created after 1978 was changed to the life of the author in addition to 50 years to the heirs after the author's death, thus eliminating the renewal system for such works. As to corporate ownership, copyright protection extends to 75 years from date of publication. The new law created also a Copyright Royalty Tribunal to deal with compulsory licensing for public broadcasting, cable television and juke boxes. In addition, the new law introduced and confirmed several concepts:

(A) the concept of "fair use," a 19th century court created rule of reason (Section 107). Fair use as a doctrine has been a part of our copyright case law since 1841. It was introduced first by Justice Story in Folsom v. Marsh, and is basically a "rule of reason" in using copyrighted work. It was left to develop as a judicial interpretation for many years, until the 1976 revision of the copyright law when it was included in our present law in Section 107. The inclusion represents a legislative endorsement of the well established doctrine. The Section stated the doctrine as it stands without any changes. The doctrine is based on the assumption that if the use of copyrighted material is reasonable and contribute to the advancement of knowledge, then the use is likely to be fair and not in violation of the author's rights. In determining whether a use is fair, one must take into account four principle criteria: (1) *the purpose of the use* is one of the determining criteria in this respect. For example, the use of copyrighted material for commercial purposes is often considered unfair and the author of the work might be entitled to control such use and to collect royalty. In considering the purpose, the copyright law cites six instances of what might be regarded as examples of fair use, such as: criticism, comment, news reporting, teaching, scholarship and research. As such, other uses might also be considered fair, provided certain criteria are satisfied. For example, though not listed in Section 107, the Senate in its 1975 Report considered audio-taping as a free service for the blind, and copying for preservation purposes, as examples of fair use. (2) *The nature of the copyrighted work* may also determine whether the use is fair or unfair. For example, work books, exercise books and standardized tests are created to be used and consumed. Therefore, any other uses that might preclude their consumption, such as reproducing them, is considered unfair. (3) *The extent of the use* is an additional important criteria in deciding whether the use is fair or unfair. The substantiality of the use might be considered in terms of its amount (e.g., number of words or number of pages). It might also be considered in terms of proportion to the original work. For example, copying one page from a one hundred page article is 1% of it; copying one page from a one page article is 100% of it. The latter use might be considered unfair. (4) *The effect of the use on the value of the work* is the last criteria to be satisfied in determining fair use. Any use of copyrighted work that might have an adverse effect on its market or on its potential value is most likely to be considered unfair. Therefore, any use that might result in a substitution or partial substitution for the original work, is not likely to be considered fair (e.g., copying chapters from a textbook which is prepared primarily for the educational market and distributing the copies free of charge to students in class, will adversely affect the marketability of the textbook).

One has to consider two factors in relation to fair use. *First*, all the above mentioned four criteria has to be proven positive. Satisfying anything less than the four criteria will not make fair use available as a defense in any questionable use. The *Second* factor is that the only authority that can determine whether one's use is fair or otherwise, is the court which will rely in its decision upon the circumstances in each case and upon the aforementioned four criteria. The unfortunate fact, however, is that fair use is a vague and ambiguous concept. It is not an absolute rule and it is unadvisable to draw an analogy from one situation to another. A decision made in any case of fair use, pertains only to this specific case under its given circumstances. One, therefore, has to look at the doubtful use from the copyright owner's viewpoint and decide whether the latter would have a reasonable objection to such use. It is rather advisable to consult an attorney if the potential adverse consequences of an error are substantial.

(B) The new law introduced also the specific provisions pertaining to library photocopying and use of copyrighted works (Section 108). This Section applies only to libraries which have their collections accessible to the public or to researchers in their specialized holdings, and that the reproduction of copyrighted material is made for no direct or indirect profit. Therefore, if the collection of a library is not accessible to the public (e.g., some corporations do not allow outside researchers to use their libraries due to confidentiality in relation to defense contracts or due to commercial competition) such library cannot benefit from the provisions of Section 108. In the meantime, the author is of the opinion that accessibility means freedom to search the collection and/or freedom to use it (e.g., reading and copying). Therefore, if a library collection is not physically available to the public but electronically accessible through, for example, a data base, then one might argue that the said library might benefit from the provisions of Section 108.

(C) The new law confirmed also that copyright protection should not be available to any work of the federal government. This denial is based on the fact that our government is a representative democracy and since it is a government by the people, society at large owns any work produced by the federal government. However, this brings to the fore a question about the federally funded research projects and the ownership of their output such as final reports. Federally funded research might be considered a work made for hire and as such the employer/the government owns the copyright on the work produced by the hired/funded person. Since the federal government cannot claim copyright on any work, it cannot assign what it does not have to others. Nevertheless, this author is of the opinion, that the conditions, in such work-relationship are governed by what the two parties agreed upon including whether or not the work is made for hire. Therefore, if the parties agreed in writing that the research project is not work made for hire, then such agreement might allow the researcher to own the copyright on the final reports, which is usually subject, in many instances, to certain provisions (such as the federal government might fund a research project provided that the principle investigator own the copyright on the final report for no more than five years and/or the investigator allows the Federal Government to use the results of the research free of charge for a limited or unlimited period of time). Therefore, it behooves the researcher to come to an agreement with the federal government or any of its agencies in writing as to the terms that will govern the final product as it relates to copyright.

The new revised law has liberalized also the strict requirements and formalities of the copyright notice. As it stands now, the omission of the notice (i.e., © or the abbreviation "copr.") does not result in the forfeiture of statutory copyright protection provided that the unintentional omission is corrected within 5 years. The revision included also a provision that would have abolished automatically the Manufacturing Clause in 1982. The Clause deals with works in the English language produced abroad by U.S. citizens/residents. Initially the Manufacturing Clause was included in the 1891 revision of the copyright law to protect American printers against the competition of what was claimed to be cheap printing abroad. Though the Manufacturing Clause's deadline was extended to July 1986, there are bills in the Congress that might extend it again indefinitely. President Reagan's veto to its extension in 1982 was, however, overridden in Congress due to the strong lobbying of the American printing industry, which argues massive loss of jobs as a reason for extending the Manufacturing Clause. Regardless of the fact that national studies have proven that the loss of jobs will be insignificant and that the American Library Association and the publishing industry are in favor of its abolishment, the strong lobbying by the American printers in an election year will probably prevail regardless of the disadvantage of retaining a concept that had outlived its purpose. In fact, some believe that the Manufacturing Clause is counterproductive and is an obstacle to international relationships.

Despite the total revision of the copyright law, the Congress fell short of dealing with the issues relating to computers and technology in general. To wit, Section 117 of the new law preserved in essence the protection status quo of information systems and reflected the congressional lack of sufficient knowledge, at the time of passage, to deal with the technological issues. Therefore, a National Commission on New Technological Uses of Copyright Work (CONTU) was created to look into the questions relating to interlibrary loans, computer software and data basis. CONTU was instrumental in its three years existence in (1) securing an agreement on guidelines between copyright owners (e.g., publishers and authors) and librarians as what is permissible copying for interlibrary loan purpose and what constitute an "aggregate quantity" of copies received through interlibrary loans that are not permissible (i.e., anything beyond 5 copies of one title within a year are not permissible or free). (2) CONTU recommended to the Congress that computer software should be accorded statutory copyright protection. As a result of the aforementioned recommendation, the Congress amended the copyright law, in 1980, by including software under the category of "literary works" (Section 102). It amended also section 117 to include certain provisions to allow the purchaser of any software to modify it to fit the intended use of it and to copy it for preservation purpose.

In passing the new revised law, the Congress acknowledged in its Report that the concept of "Fair Use" is vague and eludes precise definition and that the parties involved should come to an agreement as to what constitute fair use of copyrighted material. As a result, representatives of publishers, authors and an Ad Hoc Committee of Educational institutions and Organization on Copyright Law Revisions met several times and agreed on guidelines for classroom copying of copyrighted works for nonprofit educational institutions. It is deemed permissible under these guidelines for a teacher or his/her agent (e.g., librarian) to make one copy of a copyrighted work for research/teaching or preparation thereof. Multiple copying for classroom use is allowable only if it meets the tests of brevity, spontaneity and cumulative effect. Similar guidelines were reached with music educators and later with educators in general regarding the taping off the air of copyrighted programs for educational purposes. These different guidelines, however, are not a part of the copyright law and are technically not enforceable. On the other hand, they will carry a substantial weight in litigation since the Congress included them in the House Report and considered them to be representative of the legislative intent regarding "Fair Use." While the CONTU guidelines for interlibrary loans are applicable to all types of libraries, the guidelines for educational uses of copyrighted material are only applicable to libraries in nonprofit making educational institutions.

CURRENT ISSUES OF CONCERN TO INFORMATIONAL PROFESSIONALS

Reproduction and Distribution of Copyrighted Material

The copyright law (Title 17) states that the librarian's right to reproduce and distribute copies of copyrighted material extends only to the isolated and unrelated production or distribution of a single copy of the same material on separate occasions (Section 108d). Therefore, the librarian is not permitted to engage in multiple copying of the same material if the librarian or other members of the library staff have reason to believe that they are doing the same. The "one copy at a time rule" is extended only to libraries. The author is of the opinion that the said rule exemplifies fair use as practiced by librarians. Consequently, substantial and/or multiple reproduction of a copyrighted work is not considered fair and therefore, is not permitted. The "one copy at a time rule" does not extend to the parent institution which the library serves. The former's copying practice is governed by sections 106 and 107 and not by section 108 of the copyright law.

Though there are numerous court decisions regarding the violation of copyright through duplication of protected material, it was not until 1972 when for the first time a library was sued for copyright infringement. Williams and Wilkins, a medical journals publisher in Bethesda, Maryland, sought damages for copyright infringement, in the U.S. Court of Claims, based on photocopying as practiced by the National Library of Medicine (NLM) and the National Institute of Health (NIH). Several arguments were raised by the defendants (NLM and NIH): (1) Whether Williams and Wilkins owns proprietary rights on the articles being copied?, (2) Whether or not library photocopying (with no intended profit) violates copyright?, and (3) Whether or not photocopying by libraries is "fair use?" On February 16, 1972, Commissioner James Davis of the Court of Claims decided in favor of Williams and Wilkins stating that the copyright law (1909 Copyright Act) does not excuse libraries from liability for the kind of copying "practiced by the defendants." In appealing, the full Court of Claims ruled on November 27, 1973 in favor of the defendant library by a close vote of 4-3, based on "fair use." The finding was premised on a balancing of three tenets: (1) Williams and Wilkins did not show substantial harm resulting from the photocopying in question (2) The medical science would be seriously harmed if NLM and NIH photocopying would stop, and (3) The court would not put any risk or harm on medical science during a period when the copyright law was being reviewed by Congress. Nevertheless, the Williams and Wilkins Company took their case to the U.S. Supreme Court where the appellate decision was once more affirmed in favor of the library by an equally divided court (4-4 vote).

One has to realize that the Supreme Court decision in this case predated the enactment of our current copyright law and that the Court did not want to get involved in accommodating competing interests at the time when legislative guidance was in the making. Libraries should note, however, that NLM is a unique national library which is not analogous in mission or scope to any other type of library. A deduction based on perceived similar library practice is false and misleading. Furthermore, the equally divided Supreme Court issued in essence no opinion in the Williams and Wilkins case, thus rendering its decision a legally nonbinding precedent in future cases. Also, "fair use" cases are judged individually and every case is determined on its own merits. Therefore, it behooves the librarians to observe the law as it stands, and in the meantime lobby for its amendment if it is deemed necessary from their professional viewpoint.

Interlibrary Loans

The Library's right of copying and distribution as stated in Section 108d does not extend to cases where the library "engages in systematic reproduction or distribution of single or multiple copies" of copyrighted material. Though "systematic reproduction" is not formally defined, the term does not seem to relate to the library's "system" of handling copying requests from its own patrons. Rather, the clause seems to be intended for interlibrary loans' transactions that might substitute photocopies for subscriptions or purchase. In discussing the copyright bill in 1975, the Senate Judiciary Committee supported such interpretations by stating in its Report that systematic reproduction and distribution can be seen when a library makes copies of copyrighted material available to other libraries to the effect that the reproducing library becomes their source of such material, thus resulting in substituting these copies for subscription or purchase. However, sensing the potential crippling effect on interlibrary loans and networking, the Congress added a proviso (108g2) allowing a library to receive copies through interlibrary loan if the said library does not receive these copies in such aggregate quantities as to substitute for subscriptions/or purchase. Realizing the difficulty in defining an "aggregate quantity" in this context, the Congress asked the National Commission on New Technological Uses of Copyrighted Works (CONTU) to develop a working definition of an "aggregate quantity" and to report to the Congress on the same. After several meetings, and with the concurrence of representatives of librarians, authors and publishers, CONTU developed a set of guidelines interpreting the above mentioned term in relation to interlibrary loan photocopying. In summary, the guidelines allow a library to receive five photocopies per calendar year from periodicals published in the last five years, provided that the requesting library states in writing that it is in compliance with section 108g2 and with the aforementioned guidelines. The same applies to books with one exception that the library receives no more than five photocopies per year per title for as long as the book is protected by copyright. Nevertheless, the guidelines allow the requesting library to disregard the "rule of five" if the library has a subscription or purchase in force or on order. The guidelines also require that the requesting library must retain its records for interlibrary loans for three calendar years.

Three important points need to be emphasized in this respect: (1) Though the above mentioned guidelines are not a part of the copyright act (PL94-553) the mere fact that they were acknowledged by Congress as representing the legislative intent in Section 108g2 and are included in the September 29, 1976 Conference Report, lends considerable weight to their importance and applicability in interlibrary loan photocopying transactions (2) The said guidelines are not limiting and are not an end in themselves, because they deal with an evolving situation that will undoubtedly require continuous reevaluation and adjustment (3) The "rule of five" applies only to interlibrary loan photocopying and the CONTU guidelines in general are only applicable to libraries that are governed by Section 108 (i.e., not for profit and open to the public).

It is interesting to note that publishers are now not totally happy with the guidelines they have previously agreed upon. Based on the claim that all copyright guidelines are presently insufficient, the publishers believe that additional regulatory measures are necessary. There is reason to believe, for example, that the publishers would like to reduce the permissible five interlibrary loans copies to two. Whether such a notion will be agreed upon by the parties involved, remains to be seen.

The Five-Year Review

The current U.S. Copyright law (Title 17 USC) has a mandate in Section 108(i) requiring that the Register of Copyright review the accomplishments of Section 108 (which pertains to Library and Archives photocopying) and submit to the Congress every 5 years a report about such accomplishments and that the Report might include suggestions. Based on a commissioned national survey and on open meetings during the annual conventions of several national associations such as American Library Association, American Chemical Society, Association of American Publishers, the staff of the Office of Copyright listened to testimonies presented by educators, library users, librarians, publishers and authors regarding their assessment of the situation after the implementation of the 1976 revised copyright law. On January 3, 1983, the Register of Copyright submitted to the Congress the first Report on what was called "his best judgment about possible solutions to the copyright issue relating to libraries." The Report included "Nonstatutory" and "Statutory" recommendations. The former, includes recommendations such as negotiating "new collective library agreements" between libraries and copyright owners and "new guidelines" in light of the new technology and the present photocopying practice in libraries. The Report suggested adding a surcharge to copying equipment and presumably passing the proceeds to the copyright owners. It recommended also a study to examine the impact of technology on library use of copyrighted material and another national study to approximate the number of photocopies made on equipments in different institutions and in different locations which might help in establishing a system of compensation for the copyright owners. The nonstatutory recommendations ended by calling the government's attention to helping publicly funded libraries to enable them to pay the recommended royalties and fees. The statutory recommendations included such suggestions as the enactment of an "Umbrella Statute" which limits the penalties for infringement provided that both the library and the owner of copyright (e.g., publishers) join a "qualified licensing system." One might assume that the recommendation was suggested to boost the membership of the Copyright Clearance Center. The statutory recommendation suggested also that libraries through the amendment of Section 108, should be compelled to reproduce the copyright notice every time they photocopy a copyrighted work. Finally, the Report made it clear that the balance between the copyright owner rights and the libraries has not been achieved in practice. It referred also to evidences which prove that 25% of the photocopying done by libraries exceeds what is permitted by law. The writer is of the opinion that the 5 year Review Report has proposed a balance for the publisher's interest at the expense of the libraries statutory privileges. The Congress will have to act on the said Report sometime in the near future. It seems, at the time of this printing, that the parties involved are not concerned enough to pressure the Congress to act promptly one way or the other. What will happen, however, remains to be seen and needs to be watched closely due to the importance of the Report and its serious implications to librarianship.

Technology

Technology is another issue with great implications to copyright and libraries. Our present copyright law passed the Congress in 1976 virtually without any new provisions concerning the emerging technology. Section 117 maintained the status quo and the National Commission on New Technological Users of Copyrighted Works (CONTU), as noted previously, was created and asked among other things to look into the question regarding technology (e.g., computer software, and data bases). Many points for and against the copyrightability of computer software were argued. (See following article by Arthur Levine for more information about this subject.)

However, in 1979 CONTU presented the Congress with its final report in which it recommended extending statutory copyright protection to computer software. In 1980, the Congress passed an amendment to section 101, 102 and 117 in which computer software would enjoy the same copyright protection in the category of "literary works." The amendment allows the user of lawfully owned software to adapt it for the purpose of its intended use and to duplicate it for archival purposes. Though there are few court decisions regarding computer software, this area of copyright will need to be developed through litigation and case law.

Furthermore, to prohibit computer chip piracy, the Congress passed also in 1984, the Semiconductor Chip Protection Act which for the first time in the world created a new form of industrial intellectual property and explicitly protected the patterns on semi-conductor chips against unauthorized reproduction. The Act grants ten-year proprietary protection to "mask works" for semiconductor chips product and authorize the use of an Ⓜ as a notice of copyright on such chips. The Congress opted for a unique (sui generis) rather than a copyright approach to protect computer chips and incorporated the above mentioned provisions in the Federal District Court Organization Act, which was signed into a law (PL 98-620) on November 8, 1984. One has to realize that the said law covers only the "mask work" itself and not the computer program on the chip. The latter is protected under the copyright law (PL 94-533).

Nonprint Material

Another issue of concern to librarians is the reproduction and use of audio-visual work/nonprint material. The current copyright law is clear in that the librarians' right to reproduce copyrighted material according to Section 108, Subsection (h) does not apply to audiovisual work in general other than works dealing with news. The aforementioned provision raised a number of questions as to the use of audiovisual work in classroom teaching and to off-the-air-taping. Since the law is silent in this respect and since the Congress has encouraged all parties to discuss issues of concern among themselves, representatives of audiovisual professionals, teachers and producers of media met several times over a two-year period to resolve their differences. On September 28, 1981, they agreed upon guidelines for "Off-Air Taping for Educational Use" which were presented to the House of Representatives and were officially recognized by insertion in the *Congressional Record* on October 14, 1981. The guidelines permit taping-off-the-air for educational purposes at nonprofit educational institutions. The recorded tape can be used once by the teacher in class teaching within 10 days of the date of recording. The recorded tape can be retained by the institution for evaluation purposes for no more than 45 calendar days after which time it must be erased. The consensus is that these guidelines are representative of the spirit of fair use because they represent an appropriate balance between the rights of the copyright owner and the instructional needs of educational institutions.

The question, however, remained unsolved as to whether an individual can record off the air a program for his/her own enjoyment at a later time. The issue was brought to the attention of the court when Universal City Studios Inc. sued Sony Corporation of America for producing video recording equipment (i.e., Betamax) which is capable of reproducing copyrighted programs off the air. In January 17, 1984, the U.S. Supreme Court, in a close decision, held that noncommercial home video taping of television programs does not constitute copyright infringement, and that such home taping is generally done for the purpose of "time-shifting" for later viewing, and thus is a legitimate fair use. The court found also that the manufacturing and selling of video tape recorders to the general public does not constitute contributory infringement. Though the decision permits home video taping, it does not extend the same to libraries unless they are a part of nonprofit making educational institutions; provided that they abide by the conditions of the above mentioned guidelines in the previous paragraph. Public, special and for profit educational libraries must therefore acquire permission before taping and using off the air programs unless the latter deal with news.

Data Bases

Another current issue of concern to librarians is the legal nature of data bases and the legal implications of their use, mainly the "downloading" phenomena. A data base might be defined as a collection of information which was selected, arranged, sequenced and stored in such a way to be easily accessible to a user through the use of a computer. When one examines the current copyright law, one will find out that it did not deal with data bases. The issue, however, was referred by the Congress to CONTU for an answer. In its final report to the Congress, CONTU recommended that a data base is nothing more than a compilation which might be protected by copyright under the category of literary works (Section 102) such as dictionaries and encyclopedias. Compilations are subject to copyright because they are arranged in such a way that the resulting work, as a whole, constitutes an original work. Though the component parts of a compilation may be copyrighted individually, the compilation as a whole has its own separate copyright which extends only to the format and the arrangement of its component parts. The view is that such reformatting is an original effort without which the user would not be able to search the data easily. Conversely, the copyright on the compilation as a whole does not extend to its component parts. (See following article by Arthur Levine for further information about this subject.)

Data bases could be numeric (e.g., IP Sharp) bibliographic (e.g., OCLC) or textual (e.g., LEXIS). Regardless of their nature, data bases involve three different entities: the producer (e.g., Chemical Abstracts), the service supplier (e.g., OCLC) and the user (e.g., any library or firm). The user signs a contract with the producer or most often with the service supplier, to use the data base. Payment for the service is based mainly on connect-time in addition to other charges. Some subscribers may search a given file and download/transfer some or all of its data to the memory of their own microcomputer. This is usually done to create a personal data base or a subfile and thus save money, because it eliminates or minimizes future connect-time with the main data base. Since it implies loss of revenues to the producer and the service supplier in addition to possible violation of proprietary rights, downloading is an issue of concern to all parties involved and it raises several questions. First: who owns the data base? Obviously, if the base is created by a producer such as Biological Abstracts, then the latter owns it and can obtain a copyright on it. One has to watch, however, for the very unique situation when the service supplier and not the creator of the data, claims a copyright on the data base. In this situation, and unless there are agreements to the contrary, the copyright pertains only to the formatting and not the content of the data base. A case in point is the OCLC claim of copyright on its bibliographic data base. It is a fact that OCLC files are mainly the Library of Congress MARC Tapes which contains catalog/bibliographic information acquired by the Library of Congress, and as such it is in the public domain because it is a United States Government's works (Section 105 of Copyright Law). The remaining part of the OCLC data base is the bibliographic/cataloging data created at any given local library in fulfillment of an agreement with OCLC to input such data in the file if the latter did not contain the item and the local library has to originally catalog the said item. This part of the OCLC file is owned by the local libraries that provided it. OCLC, however, claimed copyright on its file thus creating a heated debate as to the ownership of the data file. One has to realize that OCLC copyright pertains only to the format of its data file and not to its content which is mainly in the public domain or owned by the local libraries. Some of these libraries have already claimed ownership to their own original cataloging which represents the records contributed by them to the OCLC data base (e.g., Cleveland Public Library).

The second question relates to whether downloading is in violation of copyright law. Unless there is an agreement to the contrary, downloading might be considered a violation of the copyright law. However, since downloading is hard to monitor much less to detect, data base producers are, at this point, relying on different contractual agreements for control and/or permitting their subscribers to download at a price.

The author is of the opinion that downloading might be considered "fair use" under certain circumstances. In this respect, the purpose of downloading is very important. Downloading for noncommercial teaching and research, provided the downloading data is erased from the computer memory after the research project is over, might be permissible as fair use. The nature of the original data file might also be considered in deciding whether downloading is fair or unfair. A specialized data base with limited market might be judged differently from one that is mass marketed. The same is true with regard to the substantiality of the downloaded data. The criterion in this respect is a matter of relativity since there is no definitive or permissible fair amount of downloaded data. Finally, the hardest criterion to satisfy in fair use is the effect of downloading on the actual and potential market of the data base.

Since fair use is ambiguous, negotiations and agreements, particularly collective ones, are advisable. The issue, however is complicated and will not have an easy answer in the foreseeable future.

CONCLUSION

These are some of the issues that should concern library and information managers at the point of this writing. To be informed about the copyright law, because of its serious implications to their professional objectives and functions, library and information managers should update their knowledge and watch its development in the future.

Copyright is a dynamic issue which will remain with us for as long as anyone can tell. The issue was complicated recently by the emergence of computers and the controversy they provoked will continue to intensify with the fast advancement in technology. Nevertheless, as the basis of any potential solution, our own democratic system preserves its slow legislative and judicial process by trying to solve a twenty-first century problem with a nineteenth century concept and law. In this writer's opinion, the only practical and possible solution is in the hands of the parties involved and in their willingness to adjust conflicting viewpoints for the benefit of the advancement of science and the useful arts and for the interest of the general public.

REFERENCES

Brooks, Daniel T. and Gilburne, Miles R., co-chairmen, *Contesting computer disputes: litigation and other remedies in contract, trade secret and copyright cases*. New York: Law and Business Inc., Harcourt Brace Jovanovich, © 1981.

Brooks, Daniel T. and Keplinger, Michael S., co-chairmen, *Computer programs and databases: perfecting, protecting and licensing proprietary rights after the 1980 copyright amendments*. New York: Law and Business Inc., Harcourt Brace Jovanovich, © 1981.

Circular R. 21. "Copyright and the Librarian," Copyright Office, Library of Congress, (U.S. Government Printing Office: 1977-261-023/39).

Cole, John. "Public Lending Right: A Symposium at the Library of Congress," Appendix to *Library of Congress Information Bulletin*, Vol. 42, No. 50, December 12, 1983.

"Copyright," *Encyclopedia Britannica, Macropedia*. Vol. 5, Chicago: Britannica, 1983, pp. 152-157, D.L.La.

Henry, Nicholas, Ed. *Copyright, Congress and Technology: The Public Record*, Volumes I, II, III and IV, Phoenix: Oryx, 1978.

House Report No. 94-1476 (as corrected in the Congressional Record, daily edition), Vol. 122, No. 143, September 21, 1976. p. H10727 and 10875.

Hutchings, Mary. "Model Policy Concerning College and University Photocopying for Classroom, Research and Library Reserve Use," in *College and Research Libraries News*, Vol. 43, No. 4, April 1982, pp. 127-133.

Johnston, Donald F. "Copyright handbook," New York: Bowker, 1978.

Kaufman, Benjamin S., "Copyrighting Object Code: Applying Old Legal Tools to New Technologies," *Computer-Law Journal*, Vol. 4, Fall 1983, pp. 421-440.

Kent, Allen and Harold Lancour. *Copyright: Current Viewpoints on History, Laws, Legislation*, New York: Bowker, 1972.

Ladd, David. "Private Use, Public Policy: Copyright and Home Recording," in *Wilson Library Bulletin*, Vol. 56, No. 4, December 1981, pp. 266-271.
"Manufacturing Clause Extension Basis," in *Copyright Management*, Vol. V, No. 7, July 1982, pp. 6-8.
Martyn, John, "Software Protection, Piracy and the Library . . . A Discussion Paper," *Aslib*, Vol. 13, No. 1, January 1985, pp. 13-19.
McCormick, Marilyn G., Compiler. *The Williams and Wilkins Case*, Vol. 1, New York: Science Associates, 1974.
Miller, Jerome. *U.S. Copyright Documents: An Annotated Collection for Use by Educators and Librarians*, Colorado: Libraries Unlimited, 1981.
Nasri, William Z. "A Balancing Act: Can Librarians and Users Afford It." *Journal of Library Administration*, Vol. 4, Summer 1983, pp. 11-16.
Nasri, William Z., "Crisis in Copyright," New York: Dekker, 1976.
Niblett, Bryan, "Copyright Aspects of Legal Databases," *Jurimetrics Journal*, Vol 20, No. 1, Fall 1979, pp. 30-40.
Osborne, Larry N. "Downloading Overview," *Journal of Library Administration*, Vol. 6, No. 2, Summer 1985, pp. 13-21.
Reed. Mary Hutchings and Debra Stanck, "Library and Classroom Use of Copyrighted Videotapes and Computer Software," *American Libraries*, February 1986.
Risher, Carol, "How Publishers and Librarians Can Agree on Copyright," in *Wilson Library Bulletin*, Vol. 57, No. 3, November 1982, pp. 232-233.
Snyder, Fritz, "Copyright and the Library Reserve Room," *Law Library Journal*, 1980, Vol. 73, No. 3, pp. 702-714.
Sony Corporation v. Universal City Studios, Inc., 104 S. Ct. 774 (1984).
Stratford, Juri, "Library Photocopying: A Legislative History of Section 108 of the Copyright Law Revision of 1976," *Government Publications Review*, 1984, Vol. 11, pp. 91-100.
Warrick, Thomas S. "Large Databases, Small Computers and Fast Modems . . . An Attorney Looks at the Legal Ramifications of Downloading," *Online*, Vol. 8, No. 4, July 1984, pp. 58-70.
Wolfe, Mary, "Copyright and Machine Readable Databases," in *Online*, Vol. 6, No. 4, July 1982, pp. 52-55.

Proprietary Rights in Data Bases and Software

Arthur J. Levine

> Copyright is the Cinderella of the law. Her rich older sisters, Franchises and Patents, long crowded her into the chimney-corner. Suddenly the fairy godmother, invention, endowed her with mechanical and electrical devices as magical as the pumpkin coach and the mice footmen. Now she whirls through the mad mazes of the glamorous ball. (Chafee, *Reflections on the Law of Copyright,* 45 Col. L. Rev. 503 (1945)).

The new technologies that have been developed since the Second World War have produced staggering changes for both creators and users of intellectual property. For example, Professor Chafee's whimsical statement concerning the "magical" mechanical and electrical devices preceded by several years the first functional, commercial computer. Even a scholar as prescient as Professor Chafee could not have imagined that the computer would transform society in the last half of the twentieth century much as the invention of movable type and the steam engine had transformed the world in earlier centuries. The magic of the pumpkin coach and the mice footmen is less astonishing to a generation now able to accomplish once Herculean tasks merely by pushing a few buttons on a keyboard.

Although the last two decades have seen the emergence of new technologies of wondrous scope, each age has produced its own new technologies which allow the gifted to express themselves in unique and creative ways. For instance, as a result of the development, miniaturization and sophistication of computer technology, the online bibliographic database, compact disc read-only memory (CD-ROM) and text retrieval software, most of which were once merely pumpkins and mice in most people's minds, have now been or soon will be transformed into the coach and footmen of the modern library.

Arthur J. Levine, JD (Columbia), is Counsel to the Washington, DC law firm of Finnegan, Henderson, Farabow, Garrett & Dunner and an Adjunct Professor of Copyright at Georgetown University. He was formerly Executive Director of the National Commission On New Technological Uses of Copyrighted Works (CONTU). He presently serves as the chairman of the Copyright Committee of the American Intellectual Property Law Association and as the Proprietary Rights Counsel to OCLC.

Perhaps the most creative products of the computer age are the software programs which permit computers to perform wondrous acts. In the early generations of computers, programs were created for and capable of performing only on single-purpose machines. The physical restrictions imposed upon copying such single-purpose programs apart from the computer, and the limited use of such programs, provided sufficient protection against widespread illegal copying. Today the format and use of programs is radically different. Most programs are stored on chips, disks, or tapes, and are compatible with numerous computers.

Just as computers have become consumer items, so too have the programs used on computers. Programs which may have been months and years in development can now be reproduced quickly, cheaply, and in large quantities. As stated by the National Commission on New Technological Uses of Copyrighted Works ("CONTU"):

> [I]f the cost of duplicating information is small, then it is simple for a less than scrupulous person to duplicate it. This means that legal as well as physical protection for the information is necessary incentive if such information is to be created and disseminated.

COPYRIGHT PROTECTION FOR COMPUTER PROGRAMS

In the mid-1960s, the United States Copyright Office announced that it would register claims to copyright in computer programs under the 1909 Copyright Act as "books" if "the elements of assembling, selecting, arranging, editing, and literary expression . . . are sufficient to constitute original authorship." From 1964 through the end of 1977, copyright claims in fewer than two thousand programs were registered.

The 1976 Copyright Act, which became effective on January 1, 1978, did not specifically provide protection for computer programs.[1] The legislative history of the Act makes clear, however, that Congress believed computer programs to be copyrightable from the outset as "literary works," under Section 102(a) of the Act, "to the extent that they incorporate authorship in the programmer's expression of original ideas, as distinguished from the ideas themselves."[2] This "idea-expression" distinction was made explicit in the 1976 Act in Section 102(b):

> In no case does copyright protection for an original work of authorship extend to any idea, procedure, process, system, method of operation, concept, principle, or discovery, regardless of the form in which it is described, explained, illustrated, or embodied in such work.

Section 102(b) was specifically included in the 1976 Act to make as clear as possible the scope of copyright protection in computer programs. The report of the House of Representatives Judiciary Committee accompanying the 1976 Act states:

> Section 102(b) is intended, among other things, to make clear that the expression adopted by the programmer is the copyrightable element in a computer program, and that the actual processes or methods embodied in the program are not within the scope of copyright law.[3]

On December 31, 1974, before the 1976 Act was passed, Congress established a commission, the National Commission on New Technological Uses of Copyrighted Works ("CONTU"), to study and compile data on computer uses of copyrighted works.[4] In its Final Report, delivered to the President and Congress on July 31, 1978, CONTU recommended, among other things, that the copyright law be amended "to make it explicit that computer programs, to the extent that they embody an author's original creation, are proper subject matter of copyright." CONTU proposed that a definition be added to Section 101 stating that a computer program is "a set of statements or instructions to be used directly or indirectly in a computer in order to bring about a certain result."

The Commission further recommended that the law be amended to enable the owner of a copy of a copyrighted program to adapt or make a copy of a program for archival and other limited purposes. The recommended changes were adopted by Congress and signed into law on December 12, 1980.[5] These amendments represented the first explicit mention of computer programs in the copyright law.

The CONTU Report on computer programs contained a strong dissent by one of the Commissioners, John Hersey, who argued that computer programs in their machine-control phase should not be entitled to copyright protection. He argued that such programs communicate only with a machine and not with any human audience and were not "writings" within the meaning of Article 8, Clause 8, of the U.S. Constitution. Many of Mr. Hersey's arguments were reiterated by defendants accused of infringing copyrights in computer programs.

The first case involving computer programs under the 1976 Act raised issues which echoed in several cases thereafter. In *Data Cash Systems, Inc. v. JS&A Group, Inc.*, the court decided that a read-only-memory chip (ROM) was not a copy of the program embodied in it.[6] The court held that ROMs are utilitarian devices which are incapable of being perceived by humans. On appeal, the lower court's decision of noninfringement was upheld but the appellate court did not address the issue of copyrightability, deciding the case in favor of the defendant because the plaintiff failed to affix a copyright notice on the ROMs.[7]

The questions left unsettled by the *Data Cash* case soon were being litigated in a number of courts: Is object code protectable even though it does not communicate with humans? Is object code embodied in ROMs and other memory devices subject to protection? Should operating system programs, as well as application programs, be protected? Notwithstanding the district court's decision in *Data Cash*, subsequent cases have, for the most part, answered all of those questions in the affirmative. In *GCA Corporation v. Chance*, the court held that a program in object code was copyrightable since the object code was merely the "encryption" of the source code version of the program.[8] In *Williams Electronics, Inc. v. Artic International, Inc.*, the Third Circuit Court of Appeals found that a program for an electronic video game in object code embodied in a ROM chip was entitled to copyright protection.[9] The court recognized that if the rule were otherwise, an infringer would need only wait until a program is fixed in a machine-readable form for use with a computer before safely copying the valuable work of the programmer.

> We cannot accept . . . an unlimited loophole by which infringement of a computer program is limited to the copying of the computer program text but not to duplication of a computer program fixed on a silicon chip.

Just three days prior to the *Williams* decision, the trial court in the now-famous case of *Apple Computer, Inc. v. Franklin Computer Corp.* refused to grant plaintiff a preliminary injunction, notwithstanding clear evidence of blatant copying of Apple's program by Franklin.[10] In denying the injunction, the court questioned whether programs in ROMs and object code are copyrightable and whether operating system programs are entitled to protection. The court based its opinion, in part, on the lower court's decision in *Data Cash*. On appeal, the Third Circuit Court of Appeals reversed the lower court, finding that programs in object code are copyrightable, even though such programs do not communicate with humans. The court was unable to find any basis in the statute or in the CONTU report for the proposition that a work must be intelligible to humans in order to qualify for copyright protection. The court relied on its decision in *Williams* in finding that the Apple programs embodied in ROMs were copyrightable.

The court rejected the defendant's argument that an operating system is a utilitarian device because it directs the activities of a computer, analogizing such programs to written rules which instruct people on how to play a game.

The court also was satisfied that the definition of a computer program in the Copyright Act makes no distinction between application programs and operating system programs. The defendant argued that protecting operating system programs would restrict the use of the ideas in the programs so that others would be prohibited from creating programs which make the Apple computer perform its tasks. The court stated "if other programs can be written which perform the same function as an Apple's operating system program, then that program is an expression of the idea and hence copyrightable." The court remanded to the trial court the question of whether the operating system program was capable of being expressed in more than a limited number of ways, but the lawsuit was settled before the trial court had an opportunity to hear evidence on that issue.

Illegal copying of computer programs also takes place outside the borders of the United States, and preventing the importation of such programs is becoming a primary focus of some copyright owners. Section 602 of the Copyright Act makes unauthorized importation an infringement. Copyright owners, in conjunction with the United States Customs Service, have been able to exclude the importation of computers containing infringing programs. Enterprising copyists, however, in order to avoid the detention and confiscation of their computers, have imported computers absent the ROMs. After the computers were safely in the United States, the ROMs were placed back into the computers. The Customs Service ruled that it was outside its authority to ban the importation of ROM-less computers, since only piratical copies of copyrighted works could be excluded under its regulations, and the ROM-less computers themselves are not copyrightable subject matter.[11]

Apple Computer, Inc., however, pursued its remedies under Section 337 of the Tariff Act of 1930. Under that Section, the International Trade Commission (ITC) has the authority to exclude "unfair methods of competition and unfair acts in the importation of articles into the United States." In the case of *In re Certain Personal Computers and Components Thereof*, the ITC excluded the importation of ROM-less computers which were to be fitted with copies of Apple programs, finding the importation of such computers to be a step in the direct infringement of Apple's rights of reproduction and distribution and a contributory infringement, since only Apple programs could cause the computer to function.[12]

THE FIRST SALE DOCTRINE AND SHRINK WRAP LICENSES

The copyright owner's exclusive right to distribute copies of the copyrighted work is limited by what is known as the "first sale doctrine." This simply means that the copyright owner controls only the first sale of a particular copy of his work and may not prohibit the resale, lending, or leasing of the copy after it is sold. The first sale doctrine was recently amended to extend the exclusive right to distribute phonorecords beyond the "first sale" to commercial lending or leasing activities. Congress was concerned that unauthorized copies of phonorecords were being made through rental systems, thereby infringing the copyrighted works contained on the phonorecords.

A bill to repeal the first sale doctrine as it applies to the rental, lease or lending of computer software has been introduced in Congress. Unless the law is changed, or a copyright owner of any type of copyrighted work other than a sound recording rents or leases copies of its material, sale or other transfer of ownership of the copy results in the loss of all control over further transfers of that particular copy.

In order to control the subsequent rental and perhaps illegal copying of mass distributed software, some marketers of software have resorted to "tear open" or "shrink wrap" licenses to attempt to avoid a "first sale." The licenses are printed forms usually placed in packaging which has literally been "shrunk" around the product in a cellophane or other transparent wrapper. A typical shrink wrap license provides a clause such as the following:

> You agree to the terms of this agreement by the act of opening the sealed package. . . . Do not open the sealed package without first reading, understanding, and agreeing to the terms and conditions of this Agreement.

The license agreement also typically provides that the software remains the sole and exclusive property of the distributor or copyright owner and that the purchaser merely has the right to use the material subject to the terms and conditions outlined in the agreement.

Louisiana and Illinois have enacted laws explicitly recognizing the enforceability of shrink wrap licenses. To be enforceable under the Louisiana law, and possibly to comply with conditions imposed by other jurisdictions, a shrink wrap license for computer software must contain the following five elements:

1. a written legend or notice affixed to the package in such a manner that it is clearly and conspicuously visible upon cursory examination of the software and related packaging;
2. the legend or notice must be prominently displayed in all capital letters and in readily understandable language;
3. the legend or notice must clearly state that any use of the software will constitute acceptance of the terms of the license agreement, or

that opening the sealed package in which the software is contained will constitute such acceptance;

4. the legend or notice must clearly state that if the consumer does not accept and agree to the terms of the license agreement, he or she may, within a reasonable time, return the unused, unopened software to the seller or some other identified party for a full refund; and
5. the person acquiring the software must take such action, as is stated in the legend, to constitute acceptance and agreement to the terms of the license.

Only certain terms contained in a license agreement are enforceable under the Louisiana shrink wrap law:

- retention by the licensor of title to the copy of the computer software;
- if title has been retained, prohibition of any copying of the software for any purpose;
- limitations on the purposes for which copies can be made;
- limitations on the number of copies of the software which may be made; and
- prohibition or limitation of rights to modify or adapt a copy of the software in any way, including, without limitation, prohibitions on translating, reverse engineering, decompiling, disassembling, or creating derivative works based on the licensed software.

If title has been retained, prohibitions on further transfer, assignment, rental, sale or other disposition of that copy or copies made from it may be enforced. Finally, provisions for the automatic termination without notice of the license agreement, if any provisions of it are breached by the licensee, also will be deemed enforceable if the license is accepted by the licensee.

Notwithstanding the fact that several states have passed laws specifically recognizing the enforceability of shrink wrap licenses, the validity of such licenses remains questionable. Under the law, in order for a contract to exist between parties, there must be an offer and an acceptance. Many legal scholars doubt that by tearing open a package, a purchaser has assented to a confusing and technical array of legalese. Courts may find that no true agreement between vendor and purchaser exists or that shrink wrap licenses should be held unenforceable on policy grounds. Moreover, courts could find that despite the licensor's attempt to retain title to the software, the licensor's loss of possession and control over the software, coupled with the anonymity of the ostensible licensees, is tantamount to a first sale under §109 of the Copyright Act.

COPYRIGHT OF DATA BASES

The automated data base is merely a 1980s form of a type of work which has long been eligible for copyright protection in this country. Data bases are considered "compilations" under the 1976 Copyright Law. According to the definition of "compilation" in the Copyright Act, the elements which constitute authorship in a data base are the "collection and assembling of data which have been 'selected, coordinated, or arranged.'" Long before the advent of the computer the courts provided copyright protection for a variety of different forms of data bases, such as telephone books, indexes, catalogs and the like. The fixation of a data base in a medium which requires the intervention of a computer to communicate its information content does not affect the entitlement of the data base to copyright protection. A more difficult question is: What interest in a data base is being protected? The courts have gone in two different directions on this question. Some cases say that the labor and effort expended in compiling the data base is the key element in finding the data base to be copyrightable. This view has been called "the sweat of the brow" theory of protection. A second line of cases looks not at the industry of the compiler, but rather at the selection and arrangement of data as the indicia of authorship in a compilation.

The value in an automated data base lies in large part in the ease with which the data may be retrieved. As CONTU stated:

> That ease is the product of several factors: the organization of the data, the sophistication of the program which assists in the searching and retrieving, and the skill of the searcher in articulating the search criteria.

Nevertheless, the scope of copyright protection in a data base does not shimmer with clarity. The use or reproduction of single elements of data presumably would not constitute copyright infringement. On the other hand, the duplication of a substantial portion of the data base would, under most circumstances, constitute an infringement of copyright. The determination of how much is enough to constitute copyright infringement must necessarily be decided on a case by case basis with a "fair use" analysis playing an important role in assessing liability. In considering "fair use" as a defense to copyright infringement, the Supreme Court in recent decisions has held that a use of copyrighted material for commercial purposes is presumptively unfair.

One of the ways that data bases or portions thereof are reproduced is by "downloading." *Downloading takes place when a subscriber to on-line data base services electronically stores all or portions of that data base on storage media of a mini or microcomputer.* There have been no decided cases on whether downloading of proprietary data bases constitutes copyright infringement. It has been suggested that downloading may be a fair use if merely insubstantial portions of a data base are extracted and if the portions stored are not used for commercial or competitive purposes. Others have argued that downloading is merely a new technological form of reproduction and constitutes copyright infringement. *A number of data base producers and online services offer "downloading licenses" which can be obtained by the payment of an additional license fee. This method of licensing is effective since it allows the data base producer to claim a right (i.e to prevent downloading) and then affirmatively grant or license it rather than ignore the practice and run the risk of being* "estopped" *or prevented, from raising it successfully in a court of law because it had become an accepted practice.*

COPYRIGHT OWNERSHIP

The Copyright Law provides that copyright ownership vests initially in the person or persons who actually authored the work. Thus, the copyright law carries out the mandate of the U.S. Constitution which empowers Congress to pass laws providing protection for "authors" in their "writings." Although protection is initially in the author, the primary purpose of copyright is not to reward the author, but rather to secure to the public the general benefits derived from the labors of authors. The Supreme Court has stated this purpose as follows:

> The economic philosophy behind the clause empowering Congress to grant patents and copyrights is the conviction that encouragement of individual effort by personal gain is the best way to advance public welfare through the talents of authors and inventors in Science and the useful Arts.

Thus, copyright ownership and protection in general must be viewed in the context of this Constitutional purpose.

Congress has stated that if a work is made for hire, these incentives of authorship vest initially in the hiring party; the employer. The copyright law has defined, in Section 101 of the Act, two types of works which are "works for hire."

A "work made for hire" is—

1. a work prepared by an employee within the scope of his or her employment; or
2. a work specially ordered or commissioned for use as a contribution to a collective work, as a part of a motion picture or other audiovi-

> sual work, as a translation, as a supplementary work, as a compilation, as an instructional text, as a test, as answer material for a test, or as an atlas, if the parties expressly agree in a written instrument signed by them that the work shall be considered a work made for hire. For the purpose of the foregoing sentence, a "supplementary work" is a work prepared for publication as a secondary adjunct to a work by another author for the purpose of introducing, concluding, illustrating, explaining, revising, commenting upon, or assisting in the use of the other work, such as forewords, afterwords, pictorial illustrations, maps, charts, tables, editorial notes, musical arrangements, answer material for tests, bibliographies, appendixes, and indexes, and an "instructional test" is a literary, pictorial, or graphic work prepared for publication and with the purpose of use in systematic instructional activities."

A fair reading of the legislative history of the 1976 Copyright Act leads to the conclusion that the intent of Congress was to provide entirely separate and distinct rules for works created by salaried employees and those prepared on special order or commission.

Under the above definition, only certain types of specially ordered or commissioned works could be considered "works for hire" and then only if the commissioning and commissioned parties agreed in writing that the work should be considered a "work for hire." Thus, for example, under the first part of the definition, a computer program would be a work for hire if it is created by an employee who works for a software company and has created the program as part of his or her employment for that software company. Under the second part of the definition it would seem that if the programmer is an independent contractor who is commissioned to prepare the work for the software company, the resulting program would not be considered a "work for hire" since computer programs do not fall within any of the part (2) categories of works.

A number of courts have blurred the careful distinction drawn by Congress between works created within the traditional employer-employee context and those created under special order or on commission. Those courts have found that if the commissioning party exercises significant direct supervision and control over the creation and ultimate realization of the work, the resulting work is considered a work for hire under part (1) of the definition, that is, are prepared by an "employee" acting within the scope of his or her employment. Under this formulation, the factual context within which a work is created is determinative of who initially is entitled to all of the rights in the copyright. Some courts have maintained the distinction between the part (1) and part (2) definitions and ultimately the Supreme Court may have to decide this important ownership question.

COPYRIGHT NOTICE

The notice of copyright appearing on copies of a work has long been a useful tool for librarians in determining dates of publication, length of copyright term and ultimately whether a work was protected by copyright. Prior to the enactment of the 1976 Copyright Act, copyright owners argued that maintaining a copyright notice requirement would merely result in unjust forfeitures due to unintentional or relatively unimportant omissions or errors in the copyright notice. As a result of these arguments, Congress, while maintaining a requirement for placing a copyright notice on a work, substantially liberalized the harsh results stemming from omissions or imperfections in the notice.

Under §405(a)(2) of the law, a defective notice or omitted notice can be cured by registering the work in the Copyright Office within five years of first publication and by making a reasonable effort to add a notice to all copies distributed after the omission or imperfection has been discovered. The courts have faced several questions under this curative provision. First, what constitutes a reasonable effort to add notice? The courts have required that the copyright owner add the notice to all copies within his or her control. Whether such efforts need be taken with copies no longer in the possession of the copyright owner has not yet been settled by the courts. The second question which has arisen concerning the omission of notice is whether an intentional and deliberate omission of a notice can be cured. Recently in the case of *Hasbro Bradley Inc. vs. Sparkle Toys Inc.* [13] the court concluded

> The omission of notice . . . , even if deliberate . . . , was subject to cure under §405(a)(2).

As a result of the liberalization of the notice requirements, the earlier benefits derived from the copyright notice by information handlers in general and by librarians in particular are no longer completely available. Librarians, for example, cannot with any degree of certainty determine that a work is in the public domain merely because the copy in his or her possession has no copyright notice on it. This disadvantage must be weighed against the considerable benefits to authors and other copyright owners who do not forfeit valuable rights by noncompliance with a technicality.

CONCLUSION

At the beginning of this paper, copyright was called "the Cinderella of the law" because of the wondrous new methods of creativity that technologies now provide. Whether the next several generations of copyright lawyers, information handlers and librarians will look back at the wonders of the online data base and CD-ROM as pumpkins and mice or coaches and footmen is uncertain. What is certain is the difficulty and strain that all of the new technologies place on the ability of copyright owners and users in understanding and conforming practices to these new technologies.

NOTES

1. P.L. 94-553 (1976) codified as 17 U.S.C. 101 et seq.
2. U.S. Congress, House Judiciary Committee, 94th Cong., 2d Sess., 1976, H. Rept. 1476 p. 54 (hereinafter cited as House Report).
3. House Report, p. 57.
4. P.L. 93-573 (1974).
5. P.L. 96-517 (1980).
6. 480 F. Supp. 1063 (N.D. Ill. 1979).
7. 628 F. 2d. 1038 (7th Cir. 1980).
8. 217 U.S.P.Q. 718 (N.D. Cal. 1982).
9. 865 F. 2d. 870 (3d Cir. 1982).
10. 714 F. 2d. 240 (3d Cir. 1983).
11. *In re Apple Computer, Inc.*, 28 PTCJ 75 (U.S. Customs Service, March 20, 1984).
12. CCH Copyright Law Decisions 25, 651 (Int'l Trade Comm. 337-TA-140, March 9, 1984).
13. 780 F.2d 198 (2d Cir. 1980).

Contract Issues in Computer System Acquisitions

Diane Lemka Becker

The acquisition of computer components and/or systems is a necessary process for many organizations both large and small in their attempt to take advantage of services available to them by today's information technology. The available information technology has greatly changed the role and image of the library and information center. The managers of these institutions are faced with making the right decision regarding the proper combination of technology, services and price which will best suit their own individual situation, in an environment that is changing almost daily. This acquisition involves a great amount of buyer's expense, time and usually affects large parts of the organization. Because of the large commitment involved in the acquisition, and the lack of standardization in this continually changing area, the buyer should be knowledgeable about the acquisition process to maximize its success.

Many users, sophisticated and unsophisticated, having been won over by the sales team and trusting the vendor company, have relied totally on the "good will" of the vendor and have blindly signed the standard vendor form contract for computer services. Often because of unfamiliarity and apprehension, termed "technophobia" by William Hoffer, buyers have put their implicit trust in the vendor. This has often meant putting critically large parts of the organization into the hands of the computer salesmen. As a result there have been many successful computer procurements, but also many that have failed. The following are three cases where the user, by signing standard vendor contracting procedures was left with little or no protection and a failed computer system:

Case 1: Triangle Underwriters had been in the insurance business for forty years, but within three years of changing from an IBM system to a Honeywell system which never worked Triangle Underwriters was bankrupted.

Case 2: Catamore Enterprises, a successful jewelry business for over thirty years was left with poor inventory control and an inoperative com-

Diane Lemka Becker has a Masters Degree in Information Science from the University of Pittsburgh and a BS from Rochester Institute of Technology. She is currently the manager of a medical laboratory in Pittsburgh.

puter system three years after hiring IBM to automate its production control systems.

Case 3: The Glavoratorium, Inc. needed a route accounting system. NCR agreed to provide them with a system still in testing, but had never been used or programmed for route accounting. Parts of the software and hardware never fully worked and support services were inadequate. NCR maintained that under the allocation of risk provisions in the contract, most of the responsibility was Glavoratorium's.[1-2]

On the other hand, the following are three cases where the buyer was protected by specifications in their contract:

Case 4: Kevin Hegarty describes several instances regarding the system installation at the Tacoma Public Library where the presence of a contract was useful and gave the library needed leverage in gaining vendor's support following the initial installation. The vendor, having made the sale, was neglecting the library's problems regarding the installed system. The library's contract administrator sent the vendor company a telegram requesting immediate system remedies, ending the telegram with, "If system deficiencies and specifications are not remedied by January 19, 1979, National Bonding and Accident Insurance Company shall be notified by certified mail, and penalties shall be invoked."[3] Hegarty goes on to say the telegram produced desired effects and results . . . two of the vendor's top people arrived and immediately began to give attention to their system's problems.

Case 5: In a 1983 case regarding vendor misrepresentation of production scheduling software for a candy manufacturer, the judge decided that there was "probable cause" of a breach of contract. The candy manufacturer was reimbursed the amount of money originally paid for the software.[4]

Case 6: In a case involving a medical laboratory and a software vendor, the laboratory filed fraud and breach of contract against the vendor company claiming it provided malfunctioning software and failed to fix the software errors. The laboratory had in its contract specifications that such errors be fixed. The laboratory won its case regarding the breach of contract, recovering the cost of the software plus damages.[5]

In signing an unmodified form contract, all risk of a failed procurement is on the user. The standard vendor form contract is described by Davidson as a legal agreement which "promises very little other than: delivery of a collection of machinery and electronic components which will operate in an electrically satisfactory fashion according to limited published specifications."[6]

Computer system procurement falls under the Uniform Commercial Code (UCC) which governs most U.S. commercial transactions (some local variations exist). The UCC applies to "transactions in goods." In the computer procurement application a computer is considered a "good."[7]

The UCC has several sections which allow vendors to fairly place the risk of a failed computer system on the buyer. The rationale of the legislature is to make it possible for buyers to obtain products and services at lower prices. The vendor usually utilizes the following three clauses in his form contract to shift the risk of failure to the buyers:

1. Integration Clause
2. Disclaimer of Warranties Clause
3. Limitation of Remedies Clause

Careful understanding of these clauses and the rights of both parties will aid and protect the buyer.

1. *The Integration Clause* states "there are no understandings or agreements between parties beyond those specified in the written form the user is signing."[8] By this clause the vendor has no obligations beyond what is explicitly stated in the contract. Any statements or promises made by the vendor sales representative, written or oral, have no significance and are assumed to have been bargained away by the buyer. The code states "the form contract is the final and complete agreement." The vendor uses this clause to protect itself from any promise or commitment made during the sales process by a salesperson, brochure, letter, specification sheet, etc. Sometimes, the vendor contract may be drafted so narrowly that software programs, licenses, training or maintenance terms are omitted, providing the buyer with no protection in court.

The buyer can and should take advantage of the point that despite the disclaimer, any documents attached or incorporated by reference into the final agreement cannot be disclaimed by the vendor. The wise buyer can take advantage of his rights and demand that the contract include any vendor's brochures, letters, documented oral promises and specification sheets used during the pre-sale process.

2. *The Disclaimer of Warranties Clause* in the vendor form contract disclaims all warranties whether expressed or implied. The following is an example of such a disclaimer which is permitted by the UCC and honored by the courts.

> IBM does not make any express or implied warranties, including, but not limited to, the implied warranties of merchantability and fitness for a particular purpose. In no event will IBM be liable for consequential damages even if IBM has been advised of the possibility of such damages.[9]

In spite of this disclaimer, any documents or statements incorporated into the final agreement, by attachment or by specific reference, cannot be disclaimed. The knowledgeable and cautious buyer then should demand the contract include items such as "documented systems requirements," which were agreed upon and signed by both parties. System performance standards such as response time, as well as vendor performance standards regarding maintenance should also be included to protect the buyer. The buyer might wish to include also a system reliability provision in the contract to prevent future disclaimer, such as a statement regarding "system uptime."

The vendor may disclaim implied warranties, provided he does so in accordance with the UCC provisions. To disclaim implied warranties, UCC states that the disclaimer paragraph be conspicuous and specifically include the word "merchantability." Vendors translate this into the form contract by putting the implied warranty disclaimer paragraph in a separate paragraph, often in large, colored or contrasting type. The vendor may also require the buyer to initial that paragraph.

The buyer should be aware of the implied warranties and avoid the disclaimer in them if possible. The Implied Warranty of Merchantability, unless disclaimed, imposes a vendor obligation that the computer system be fit for "the ordinary purposes for which such a system is used." The Warranty of Fitness arises when the vendor "at the time of contracting has reason to know any particular purpose for which the goods are required and the buyer is relying on the seller's skill or judgment to select or furnish suitable goods."[10] This second implied warranty would be of extreme importance to a buyer who has relied strongly on a vendor study, needs assessment, system design and proposal for services.

3. *Limitations of Remedies Clause*. The third vendor form contract clause the buyer should be aware of is the Limitations of Remedies Clause. This limits the buyer's remedies when a contract is breached. Limitations may be a ceiling to the vendor's total liability, such as limiting the buyer's damage to a return of the purchase price. The policy of many lease and sales contracts from vendors such as Radio Shack regarding computer hardware is to limit remedies and liability to repair or replacement for a maximum of 90 days after delivery. Such companies eliminate all remedies regarding software acquisition. Vendors generally take special care to exclude liability regarding indirect, special or consequential damages such as lost profits caused by computer system failures.

The buyer should gain as much familiarity with the entire contract and its terms and disclaimers as he can, in order to make an agreement which will provide him with as much protection and as few surprises as possible.

As the process of computer procurement contracting matures, the role of the buyer in the contracting process is also changing. Buyers are taking a more active role in designing contracts to specifically address their individual needs, and to give them some protection and leverage in the systems procurement.

According to Davidson, standard vendor form contract fall into three categories. These categories are: the traditional approach; a systems approach and project control.

In the traditional approach the buyer treats the computer system contracting process like that of its other business procurements, relying on his/her own negotiation skills to gain some power in the system procurement process. This approach is normally practiced by large, well-managed firms for whom negotiation is a regular part of their business. The problems develop from the fact that computer contracting is not like other business acquisitions. The peculiarities of data processing must be taken into account. The buyer employing this method of contracting, unfortunately usually concentrates on negotiating areas of the contract which resemble other procurements with which he/she is familiar, such as the allocation of risk provision in the vendor form contract. In areas unique to computer/data processing contracting, the buyer ends up relying on the vendor contract terms. Therefore, the buyer who negotiates the vendor form contract is only partially closer to achieving the best procurement contract for his business.

The systems approach on the other hand, defines the procurement process in terms of functional performance of the system. The contract is approached as a document which explains the functional results the buyer wants from the final system. This form of contracting is defined by Harris, as "results contracting." In contracting for results, the buyer attempts to shift to the vendor the burden of insuring that the people, products or services supplied by the contract will actually meet both the technical specifications and the desired level of end-user service. This requires increased effort on the part of the buyer as he must determine and clearly define the document, the processing results desired by the end-user, so as to provide the vendor with a detailed written description of exactly what the system is to achieve. The buyer must define in detail "the system," how it "works," and the "end results" desired.

In systems contracting, systems analysis is applied to all aspects of the procurement. In the contract, equipment and product specifications remain important, but the main emphasis should be on how to define and describe the desired results in a binding legal agreement. The contract covers all aspects of the procurement by specifying:

1. System performance on a functional level;
2. Delivery and installation obligations;
3. Acceptance testing procedures;
4. Warranties.

This type of contract increases the vendor's liability and risk of nonperformance. A task of crucial importance is to distinguish between vendor and user responsibilities. This is not always accomplished easily, but is necessary for the success of the procurement.

Project Control is the third type of contracting described by Davidson. This builds on the same underlying concepts as a systems approach contract, that of determining and defining performance standards and incorporates the concepts of project control into the contract. Systems such as software development, that are developed and implemented stagewise, as projects, are candidates for this form of contracting. The project timetable, defining major tasks and critical completion dates is included as part of the agreement along with acceptance testing standards of each component and for the entire system, on-going support and maintenance standards and contract remedies. (Project control contracts, being a more specialized form of systems contracting, will not be covered in any further detail within the scope of this article.)

DRAFTING A SYSTEMS PROCUREMENT CONTRACT

Drafting the systems procurement contract as a "working document" is a new, complex and changing area of the law, requiring active participation of both parties and legal counsel. Following is a checklist of items which should be addressed when designing a systems acquisition contract.

Functional Specifications

The functional specifications are the most fundamental element of the contract as they clearly state the vendor responsibilities and provide the basis for acceptance testing. These specifications should be comprehensive, including:

- the transactions the software is to implement;
- performance criteria for each particular software and hardware unit(s);
- processing volumes;
- system accuracy standards;
- network characteristics, requirements for compatibility of units;
- description of what the system is to accomplish as a whole.

These specifications should be in enough detail to enable developers unfamiliar with the buyers organization to work from the specifications alone in system design and software development.

The specifications are developed beginning with an initial internal review and needs assessment by the buyer. Then the buyer technical staff and vendor work together to design specifications which will meet the buyers needs and which the vendor is capable of providing. Consulting firms outside the organization may also be used to create the functional specifications.

These specifications while providing details of vendor duties also benefit the user in the following respects:

- The user is forced to integrate the system procurement with its other data processing and business functions.
- Functional specifications educate the user as to what can realistically be expected from a computer system.
- Early in the process, the user-vendor relationship becomes defined.

SITE Preparation and Operations Requirements

Requirements and responsibilities as to space, air conditioning, humidity, electrical requirements, etc. must be clearly and explicitly stated.

Project Timetable

This is to include all deadlines the vendor is obligated to meet, as well as a description of remedies if dates are missed.

Acceptance Testing

Acceptance testing is one of the most important elements of an acquisition agreement. Harris states, "In the words of one experienced negotiator, 'If you only get one decent concession from your vendor, make it a solid acceptance test.' "[11] In certain applications one may want to consider on-going performance criteria as well.

The acceptance criteria incorporate the functional specifications previously created to describe performance tests for the equipment or products. These performance tests must be met before the buyer is liable for payment of purchase or rental price. Other contractual matters affected by acceptance date are: passage of title, risk of loss, insurance, initiation of maintenance or licensing fees.

Acceptance testing is a dynamic process and the testing time should be for a period of sufficient length to allow for one normal processing cycle of transactions and for the "burn-in" of the equipment. Software and hardware components must all be tested individually with live as well as simulated data, as well a total system testing. Hegarty recommends the following tests to comprise the minimum acceptance testing protocol of a system:

1. Hardware Quality Acceptance Test—testing system boot, CPU, all memory, all peripherals and remote communications as well as power-fail operation.
2. Database Transfer Acceptance Test—to follow the successful completion of the hardware test.
3. Software Functional Performance Acceptance Test—to confirm that software meets specifications stated in the RFP.
4. Full-Load Throughput Acceptance Test—to test the system at projected peak transaction rates.
5. System Reliability Acceptance Test—to test the integrity of the system.
6. Final Acceptance Test—the test of the system's overall, day-to-day operations for a period of 90 days.[12]

Acceptance provision criteria must be explicitly detailed in the contract since standard vendor form contracts often exclude any user acceptance provisions.

Personnel and Support Requirements

This defines the amount of training the vendor must supply, at what buyer's location; with what frequency; the number of staff to be trained and any costs involved in the training. Also defined within this area of the contract are the numbers of people at defined skill levels required to operate and maintain the system. The contract should also specify what operations manuals and systems and programming documentation the vendor is responsible to supply.

Payment Procedures

The payment schedule whenever possible should be conditional upon satisfactory completion of acceptance tests. This again must be explicitly defined in the contract, as without such contractual arrangement, payment is often due independently of any final acceptance procedures.

Davidson recommends the following payment approach:

- partial payment upon satisfactory demonstration of completed software;
- substantial payment upon completion of systems acceptance testing;
- final payment (about 10% of total price) at the completion of all remaining obligations, such as training, documentation, correcting minor problems.[13]

The contract may also include a bonus payment if the system is completed ahead of schedule.

Hardware Maintenance Terms

The system maintenance may be the most important contract element in terms of long-range functioning. In the contract, the buyer should get a supplier commitment to maintenance standards, timeliness, hours routine maintenance is performed, emergency maintenance availability, timeliness and hours performed, skill levels of maintenance personnel, guaranteed average and maximum response times in cases of hardware failure and access/availability of spare parts.

Vendor form agreements usually include a "force majeure" (acts of God) clause. The buyer's attorney should examine the clause carefully and amend it if necessary.

Software Maintenance Terms

Software maintenance is expensive, requiring the user to pay a monthly fee after the initial installation/acceptance period to cover modifications, enhancements and problems.

Special Remedies

Special remedies when written into the contract, may resolve problems without the buyer having to declare a breach of contract. The Special Remedies must offer the buyer a benefit and a cost or risk to the vendor. Some examples of special remedies from Hegarty's Tacoma Library Contract are:

> When the vendor fails to meet a specified delivery date the library is accorded the right to cancel the agreement after notice to the vendor.
>
> When the system fails to pass the benchmark performance stage of the acceptance test; upon the request of the library, the vendor is obligated to supply additional equipment within a stated period, at no cost to the library.
>
> When the equipment fails to meet the continuing performance standards during the term of the agreement; upon the request of the library, the vendor is obligated to replace the defective or inadequate component within a stated period at no cost to the library.[14]

Cancellation Provisions

Cancellation provisions define periods within which hardware and software components can be canceled, penalties for such cancellation and circumstances when the vendor can legally terminate services.

Conversion Terms

These define participation and support of the vendor during a conversion.

Patent Indemnification

This clause states that the vendor will absorb all litigation costs should disputes concerning technological ownership of the product arise.

Warranty of Products

(as discussed in detail previously)

Inclusions and Attachments to the Contract

(as discussed in detail previously) All additions and deletions to the contract should be signed and dated by both parties.

Assignments

Assignments should be included to protect both the vendor and buyer by addressing the actions to be taken in the event of the bankruptcy or sale of one of the companies (vendor or buyer) during the period of the contract.

Language of the Contract

Careful use of language in the contract is essential. General, ambiguous terms such as "turnkey," "user-friendly," "state-of-the-art" and "management information system" should be avoided as differences in their interpretations will lead to problems. To bridge the comprehension levels between the technical, legal and lay languages among the people involved in the process, emphasis, time and care should be taken to insure legal interpretations in the contract's verbiage and lay understanding and intention are all of one mind.

Negotiation

The negotiation process is a critical process in the success of an acquisition. The vendor, who has heretofore been in the "romance period" of the sales process, is now out to make the best deal possible for his company and his career. He is experienced in negotiations, wants to use his company form contract with which he is familiar and experienced. He may utilize also as many other strategies as possible to gain a much information and leverage in the negotiation process as possible.

According to Davidson, a buyer must be aware of the salesperson's dual roles and approach the process in the following manner:

- with an understanding of the negotiation process;
- with preparation;
- with an attorney(s) skilled in computer acquisition negotiations and the procurement process;
- with a business-like approach;
- will negotiate concepts before clauses;
- with flexibility and creativity.

Contract Administration

A part of the contract process often neglected is that of contract administration. Hegarty states "a contract worth negotiating is also worth administering." Contract administration involves:

1. insuring that the buyer meet his contractual obligations;
2. insuring that the vendor meet his contractual obligations;
3. providing written documentation of buyer and vendor performance;
4. insuring that the working system meets specifications.

Hegarty recommends there be a contract administrator, a published contract administration plan including schedules and timetables, definitions of responsibilities of all parties, documentation forms, vendor compliance certificates and maintenance/operations logs.[15]

It is imperative that the buyer documents all system malfunction, in addition to all received services from the vendor and the vendor's responses and outcomes. Such documentation is required for contract remedies. Also important is the timeliness and adequacy of the vendor's notification of problems. Rice suggests having notices such as rejection and revocation of acceptance drafted by an attorney as informal documentation may be insufficient in major litigation.[16]

Drafting a workable contract, equitable to all parties is a difficult task. Rice, a member of the Missouri bar, suggests that it is not practical to expect vendors to significantly alter their basic contracts for individual buyers. He recommends instead that the buyer concentrate on: (1) "sale-on-approval" contracts which allow the buyer a 90 day period in which to return the system if dissatisfied and (2) limitations on price increases for software support and accessory equipment.[17]

Sterne and Saidmain also advise that most sellers will not change their standard contract especially on single system deals. They advise buyers to protect themselves by drafting a "side letter." This letter specifically incorporates the standard agreement, but states that the modifications contained within the letter supersede the comparable terms in the seller's standard contract. Both documents must be signed and dated on the date of sale by the seller and buyer.[18]

Another factor, besides that of the vendor's willingness to change the standard contract, may be that the time pressures on the buyer. The buyer may feel pressed to get the system purchase and installation under way and in an attempt to save time, may bypass any contract modifications. This may, in the long run, prove to be more costly in terms of both time and money.

Vendors most likely will not give in to all the buyer demands suggested here, but the buyer's own drafted contract can serve as a negotiation starting point. The vendor and buyer alike must realize that with the recent saturation of the computer market, the computer industry layoffs and cutbacks, it is now a buyer's market in computer land. To make the most of his position in the market, the buyer should incorporate legal counsel, skills, business savvy, knowledge and realism.

As an author's note to this subject, I would like to emphasize item three in Davidson's above mentioned checklist . . . obtain and utilize a lawyer or lawyers who have experience and skill in the area of computer system procurement. This area is very new and complex with standards just developing. Buyers and vendors alike must rely on the experience of attorneys to help them use the laws of this area to their best advantage. To quote Alexander Gaydish, "Don't be your own lawyer."[19] This requires of the legal community a commitment to develop specialists in this area, as well as legislation.

There are also many specialized computer consultants who are willing to handle the entire system acquisition. If this is the direction your organization chooses, these individuals must be interviewed and chosen as carefully and thoroughly as vendors. Use of such a specialist however, does not negate the need for legal counsel.

Secondly, I feel the buyer himself should gain as much familiarity and knowledge as possible about the equipment or system he is purchasing, about the vendor company, and about the negotiation procedures and contract. The buyer cannot afford to blindly rely on the vendor's expertise and sales presentation.

In the conclusion of the case notes of *Triangle Underwriters v. Honeywell, Inc.*, Greg Kirchhoff states:

> What is needed to deal with future cases is a judiciary, legislature and organized bar, educated about computers. Education will aid the development of legal principles necessary to confront this booming, almost pervasive technology.[20]

In addition to calling for education of the legal community, I suggest that education of both the buyer's community and the lay community can only benefit individuals, corporations and life in a world where the "pervasive technology" has become a part of every day activities. The users and buyers must be educated about systems procurement and the laws governing it. They must take an active role in the process, enlisting legal counsel to make the contract and negotiations workable and productive so as to produce a successful acquisition.

NOTES

1. Davidson, p. 142.
2. Volz & Mumford, p. 247.
3. Hegarty, p. 48.
4. Hegarty, p. 48.
5. Hegarty, p. 49.
6. Davidson, p. 142.
7. Davidson, p. 136.
8. Volz & Mumford, p. 249.
9. Volz & Mumford, p. 250.
10. Volz & Mumford, p. 251.
11. Harris, p. 91.
12. Hegarty, p. 47.
13. Davidson, p. 146.
14. Hegarty, p. 50.
15. Hegarty, p. 48.
16. Rice, p. 492.
17. Rice, p. 491.
18. Sterne & Saidmain, p. 404-6.
19. Gaydish, p. 249.
20. Kirchhoff, p. 202.

REFERENCES

Davidson, Duncan M., "Project Controls in Computer Contracting." *Computer Law Journal*, Vol. 4, Summer 1983, pp. 133-158.

Gaydish, Jr., Alexander, *Principles of EDP Management*, Reston Publishing Co., Inc., 1982.

Golden, Bruce P., "Contracting for Computer Products," *Banking Law Journal,* Vol. 107, March-April 1985, pp. 173-177.

Harris, Charles Edison. "Complex Contract Issues in the Acquisition of Hardware and Software," *Computer Law Journal*, Vol. 4, Summer 1983.

Hegarty, Kevin, "Vendor Abandonment," *Library Journal*, Vol. 3, No. 2, Feb. 1, 1986, pp. 47-50.

Hoffer, William. "Technophobia can be good for you," *Barrister*, Vol. 12, no. 4, Fall 1985, p. 61.

Hoffman, Paul S., "Software Development and Services Agreements," *Jurimetrics Journal*, Vol. 24, Fall 1983, pp. 58-64.

Joseph, Jonathan, "Computer Contract Challenges," *Computer Law Journal*, Vol. 5, No. 3, Winter 1985, pp. 379-391.

Kirchhoffer, Greg, "The Effect of the Statute of Limitations on a Computer Vendor's Liability in a Failed Computer Installation-Triangle Underwriters, Inc. v. Honeywell, Inc., 604 F.2d 737 (1979)," *St Louis University Law Journal*, Vol. 26, December 1981, pp. 181-202.

Rice, Charles M. "Computer Law for the Non-Specialist," *Journal of the Missouri Bar*, Vol. 41, December 1985, pp. 489-491.

Sterne, Robert Greene and Saidmain, Perry J., "Computers and Law; the Sale of Computer Products," *Byte*, Vol. 10, No. 5, May 1985, pp. 399+.

Volz and Mumford, "Computer Contracts: Negotiating User Protection," *Journal of Products Liability*, Vol. 7, Summer 1984, pp. 247-254.

Zammitt, Joseph P., "Contracting for Computer Products (Part 1)." *NY State Business Journal*, Vol. 54, April 1982, pp. 128-31.

Zammitt, Joseph P., "Contracting for Computer Products (Part 2)." *NY State Business Journal*, Vol. 54, June 1982, pp. 214-218.

Zammitt, Joseph P., "Contracting for Computer Products (Part 3)." *NY State Business Journal*, Vol. 54, August 1982, pp. 294-298.

The Background of Proposed Legislation to Study Public Lending Right in the United States: Issues in Policy, Law and Administration

Dennis Hyatt

> Culture does not survive, or flourish, if we are talking about books, unless writers flourish.[1]

Despite this high approval, there is evidence that authors do not flourish. In the United States, 51 percent of authors—that is, contemporary writers who have had at least one book published—earn less than $5,000 annually from writing.[2] In Great Britain, more than half the authors earn less than half the national average income from their writing.[3]

> This recitation [of author's income statistics for various countries] could be expanded to any country in which the economic status of the author is discussed. The discussions also show that the full-time, self-employed author as the propagator and disseminator of national culture is seen as socially desirable and that he should be supported if he is not as fortunate as his best-selling colleague.[4]

In search of support, U.S. authors are now seeking federal legislation to establish a public lending right (PLR), a European concept which provides that authors be compensated for the multiple use of their copyrighted works in libraries. Public lending right is based on the premise that an author's potential for royalty income begins to evaporate when a library, having purchased perhaps just one copy of a book, lends it to an indefinite number of readers. Arguably, a person is much less likely to purchase a book if he has read a copy borrowed from the library.

Dennis R. Hyatt, JD, MLL (Washington), is Law Librarian and Associate Professor, School of Law, University of Oregon. He is the Co-Editor of the *Library Trends* issue on the "Legal Aspects of a Public Lending Right" (1981). He was an Adjunct Professor at both the School of Law and the School of Librarianship, University of Tennessee, during 1975 and 1976.

"[T]he 'labor of love' approach [to writing] is changing,"[5] and that is why authors in several countries have been working to enact PLR legislation which in some way or another would compensate for the loss of royalty earnings arising from library lending activities.

In 1973 Congressman Ogden Reid introduced the first public lending right legislation in the United States, a bill "to establish a commission to study and make recommendations on methods for compensating authors for the use of their books by libraries."[6] The proposal died in the Committee on House Administration without a hearing, and thus ended the initial tentative step for authors' royalties legislation. Following a 1983 symposium on public lending right sponsored by The Center for the Book at the Library of Congress, Senator Charles Mathias introduced a bill "to establish a commission to study and make recommendations on the desirability and feasibility of compensating authors for the lending of their books by lending institutions."[7] Again there was no action taken on the proposal which had been sent to the Senate Committee on Rules and Administration (chaired by Senator Mathias) because jurisdiction of the committee includes the Library of Congress, and the proposed National Commission on the Public Lending of Books would be created within the Library of Congress.

In 1985 Senator Mathias again introduced a public lending right bill, in this instance "to establish a commission to study and make recommendations on the desirability and feasibility of amending the copyright laws to compensate authors for the not-for-profit lending of their works."[8] The proposed National Commission on the Lending of Authors' Works is not created within the Library of Congress. The bill has been referred to the Senate Judiciary Committee, which has jurisdiction over matters involving intellectual property, where Senator Mathias is chairman of the Subcommittee on Patents, Copyrights and Trademarks.

The differences in these three bills to study public lending right extend far beyond their captions and the mechanics of Congressional committee assignment. The parts of the texts which set forth the purposes of the commission and its specific charges are different, and these differences reflect an increased comprehension of the underlying issues that any PLR scheme must address. Thus, even though no hearings have yet been held on the current bill, the current text demonstrates that Senator Mathias and his staff have a growing appreciation and understanding of the problems of policy, law, and administration that public lending right legislation will present.

The current bill provides a useful outline for discussing the recurring questions of PLR that other nations have faced. In the last 40 years, eleven nations have enacted PLR legislation: Denmark (1946), Norway (1947), Sweden (1954), Finland (1961), Iceland (1967), the Netherlands (1971), Federal Republic of Germany (1972), New Zealand (1973), Australia (1974), United Kingdom (1979), Canada (1986).[9] The PLR concept has also received considerable attention in other countries, most notably Austria, Belgium, France, Italy and South Africa.

> The idea of a public lending right . . . did not, of course, develop in a vacuum. . . . Several sets of events already in motion by the turn of the twentieth century combined to provide it with a hospitable environment: (1) the development of lending libraries (especially public libraries), (2) expansion of the copyright umbrella, (3) increasing willingness of governments to provide money from public funds for the support of cultural affairs, (4) the rising awareness (in some countries) of the need to protect and nourish a national culture and language, and (5) a growing trend toward collective activism among individuals with an identity of economic interests.[10]

The experiences of these other countries provide telling points in a review of the provisions of the current bill which will follow:

a. "*The purpose of the Commission is to consider whether specific compensation to authors for the lending of their works would promote authorship in the United States without adversely affecting the reading public.*"[11] "There is no evidence that any book has ever been written because of a PLR scheme, or that one has not been written because of the absence of such a scheme."[12] Is it asking too much of PLR schemes to show a direct causal link to promotion of authorship? Probably so. In the United Kingdom

> [the] increasing annual output of titles has been accompanied by a decline in the volume of sales per title: in the 1960s some 300 million volumes were printed annually, but in the 1970s, this figure fell to about 200 million. . . . The authors' economic welfare is inevitably conditioned by the vicious circle of ever-increasing [book] manufacturing costs firmly linked to higher prices and reduced sales. From the early 1970s library book funds have been reduced in real terms, and the trend is continuing. In these circumstances, authors are more anxious than ever to ensure that they are rewarded for the use of their books by library borrowers, as well as for the sale of their books to libraries.[13]

Perhaps, then, public lending right legislation would promote authorship more by reducing anxieties than by assuring financial gain. As author Robert Caro has noted, it may be that the "simple justice of the case" is more important than the money.[14] On the other hand, George Piternick suggests that the financial problem for most authors is not that libraries freely lend the books they purchase, but rather than not even libraries purchase the books in the first place.[15] Under this view, PLR would be an inexact, if not inappropriate, means for promoting authorship and would likely benefit those authors least in need of encouragement.

> The arguments for the public lending right are essentially couched in terms of rewarding authors who presently just cannot make a living as writers. If you followed the notion of public lending right strictly . . . and rewarded on the basis of use, you would be rewarding exactly those people who are already very highly compensated—and perhaps are entitled to more compensation—but you're not going to be rewarding the person whose book will perhaps be published, perhaps be sold to a library, but not used all that frequently.[16]

b. If it finds that a PLR scheme would promote authorship, the Commission is charged "*to make recommendations from funds to be appropriated by the Congress or from a national trust fund established for that purpose*."[17] This provision is designed to alleviate the most common anxiety of librarians—namely, that PLR schemes threaten the concept of free use of public libraries if the financial support to the author might come from government funds that would otherwise go to libraries. Public lending right is administered in the United Kingdom by the Office of Arts and Libraries, the same agency responsible for the allocation of library funds. "The [British] government will quickly forget that they said the money that was going to be available for PLR was going to be extra to what was already allocated [for libraries]."[18]

American Library Association Executive Director Robert Wedgeworth feels that librarians would support almost any legislation intended to promote authorship so long as library funding is not diminished. Approximately 95 percent of American public library funding comes from local and state sources, the remaining five percent coming from federal appropriations.[19] Thus, if a PLR scheme is federally funded, a large portion of public library funding is unaffected. This situation contrasts sharply with European PLR countries where library organization and funding are substantially more centralized at the national level, and where librarians have voiced their anxieties more pointedly in the funding debates.

c. The Commission shall "*assess the relevance to the United States of systems in operation or under consideration in foreign countries. . . .*"[20] The "sheer size" of the United States and the decentralization of U.S. libraries and educational institutions will make it much more difficult to institute a PLR system here than in the smaller and more centralized nations of Europe.[21] Indeed, compared to the total of the seven PLR countries of continental Europe, the United States has over two times the population and six times the area. Regarding public libraries, a survey by the United Nations Educational, Scientific and Cultural Organization indicates that the U.S. has over one and one-half times the number of administrative units, five times the number of service points, two and one-half times the number of volumes, and two times the number of annual loan transactions of those countries. The continental PLR countries have 0.24 fewer library books per capita but 0.41 more annual loan transactions per capita, indicating that public library resources are more intensely used in Europe.[22] Robert Wedgeworth cautions against relying on the accuracy of library statistics reported by international agencies, noting that the lack of uniform definitions is a major impediment to comparing the reported statistics of nations.[23] Nonetheless the U.S. public library community is relatively large and diffuse, consisting of approximately 8,000 libraries (excluding branches and other subdivisions), half of which serve populations of fewer than 50,000 persons.[24]

Besides being larger, the United States is without much question more culturally diverse than any one of the continental PLR countries – each of which has a different national language that contributes to its cultural unity.

> Though there is an extraordinary similarity between the Scandinavian languages, apart from Finnish, and although Swedes, Norwegians and Danes at a general level of education will easily be able to read and understand each others' languages, it is a statistic fact that there is no considerable export of books from one Nordic country to another. . . . [T]he number of English books and periodicals sold in Denmark surpasses the number of Nordic books sold in [Denmark] by several hundred percent.[25]

The social structure and the political conditions of the Scandinavian countries are probably the factors most influencing the initial development and administrative implementation of their PLR schemes.[26] "[T]hese countries are protecting their cultures from foreign (cultural) invaders by supporting native 'creators.' The movement for PLR may start out as compensation for book use . . . but there is no doubt that the end result is to protect and encourage [authorship by] their own people. . . ."[27] Perhaps PLR schemes as part of the culture industry "can be comprehended only on the basis of the interdependence of culturo-political and economico-political objectives."[28] In short, there are significant difficulties in just describing the PLR scheme of one nation in a way that is understandable and relevant to the different objectives of another nation, and the greater the differences in culture and size of the two nations, the less relevant the PLR scheme is likely to seem.

Nonetheless, all public lending right schemes are relevant in the sense they provide a variety of ideas for implementing plans. Most interest in the U.S. is currently focused on the United Kingdom because a PLR plan was recently enacted there, and because the British and Americans share a relatively close cultural identity. Still, the scheme could be called "illogical, insular, and legally isolationist . . . [but] gloriously workable."[29]

d. The Commission shall "*compile data on the various types of lending of books . . . and if it recommends the establishment of a compensation system shall . . . identify appropriate criteria for determining the amount of compensation, including the following: (i) the number of copies sold to lending institutions, (ii) the number of copies stocked by lending institutions, (iii) the number of circulations.*"[30]

The lack of factual information exacerbated the acrimony between authors' groups as well as between authors and librarians in Great Britain as the implementation scheme was debated.[31] The Senate bill foresees the problem that there is no data currently available that would provide a nationwide profile of U.S. library lending activities based on either the type of loan, i.e., in-library use or circulating, or on the type of material, i.e., reference works, fiction, children's books. Furthermore, the library and its lending services have been characterized as inimical to the interests of authors "in the absence of any significant data on the role and influence of the library market on the sale of books."[32]

In suggesting criteria for determining the amount of compensation, the Senate bill clearly anticipates looking to PLR schemes in other nations as examples, if not models, of possible compensation plans. In Australia, compensation is based on the number of copies stocked in libraries. "Payment is made annually where at least 50 copies of an eligible book are estimated to be held in public lending libraries throughout Australia. The estimate is obtained by surveying the book stock of a sample of public lending libraries selected each year by the Australian Bureau of Statistics. A survey of all books is *not* conducted, nor does the survey include libraries of educational institutions. The basic rate of payment is 60 cents per estimated copy for authors' PLR. . . ."[33]

In the United Kingdom, payment is based on the number of circulations:

> A representative sample is recorded, consisting of all loans from sixteen sample public libraries. This is then multiplied in proportion to total library lending to produce for each book an estimate of its total annual loans throughout the country. . . . The sample represents only public libraries (not academic, private, or commercial libraries), and only loans made over the counter (not consultations of books on library premises). . . . The sample consists of the entire loans record for a year in sixteen public libraries representa-

> tively spread through England, Scotland, Wales and Northern Ireland.[34]

"We now have a fully satisfactory way of calculating PLR remuneration in respect of books borrowed from public libraries. The objections to PLR being infeasible or impractical have been completely overcome by using the latest available library computing technology."[35] Perhaps. Originally, 72 library service points were scheduled for sampling to assure statistical validity, but this number steadily dropped as projected administrative costs rose.[36] Now data is collected from ten "principal" service points and six "ordinary" service points, which represents approximately 1.2 percent of all library lending. The selection of service points has focused on those libraries already using suitable computer-based systems to record book loans.[37] To counteract possible sampling errors, four of the six "ordinary" service points are changed every year. "The computer can detect abnormalities in the loans pattern in sample libraries and will reject attempts by borrowers to push the loans of a particular book to artificial heights."[38] With so few libraries in the sample, there is also potential for regional bias in the survey. "In Wales, the sample borrowings were as many as one in 50 of the total borrowing; in the Southern English counties, as few as one in 200."[39]

> If the registered interest in a book scores so few loans that it would earn less than £5 in a year, no payment is due. . . . If the books of one registered author score so high that the author's PLR earnings for the year exceed £5,000, then only £5,000 is paid. No author can earn more than £5,000 in any one year. The bottom limit operates for each edition of a book, the top limit per author.[40]

In 1984 approximately 6,000 British writers received payments on the basis of the first sample year in 1983. The royalty was fixed at 1.02p per loan, and 46 authors received the statutory maximum payment. Eighty-one additional authors each received more than £2,500; 565 received between £500 and £2,500; 1,516 between £100 and £499; and 3,878 received less than £100. "Some authors of nonfiction titles have been particularly disappointed at the smallness of their PLR payment, which confirms the generally held theory that Britain's libraries are used more for the borrowing of middlebrow novels than any other category."[41]

Thorny administrative issues may still test the British scheme. Considering the publicity surrounding the first payments, more authors may register for PLR participation, and the 1.02p per loan will fall. The Parliament has not shown any willingness to increase the £2 million PLR appropriation.[42]

The United States may find special relevance to the operation of the British system and the PLR system of West Germany (which also samples library lending as a basis for compensation). These are the only two PLR nations which provide compensation to foreign authors, rather than limit coverage to citizens and residents. However, each country requires reciprocity agreements between nations before the foreign author can benefit. It is not clear whether reciprocal treatment would mean the criteria for determining the amount of compensation, or any other provision, need be essentially the same.

e. The Commission shall "*identify procedures for determining and paying any such compensation without imposing upon the public libraries . . . burdensome administrative requirements*.[43] As with the bill's provision relating to the source of PLR funds, this section addresses a second librarian anxiety about PLR schemes—that they are expensive to administer and will divert substantial resources away from library public service. In the United Kingdom, the expenses of the Office of Public Lending Right and the costs to libraries for recording loans are charged against the government appropriation for author distribution. In 1983 these charges totaled £416,000 against the £2,000,000 fund.[44] One reason British authors do not challenge more vigorously the increased range of statistical error that is more probable with small samplings is the realization that they will directly pay for the administrative costs a larger sampling would entail.

In Norway the annual PLR government grant has no relation to library circulation or collection holdings, and there is no individual author compensation. The annual government grant equals at least five percent of the total state and local grants for the purchase of books and other materials for loan. "It appears that the 5 percent rule has been reduced to a formality, since the total government grant obtained through negotiation is about three times the legal minimum."[45] The money is divided among a number of funds and collecting societies and is used for scholarships and other social purposes. It is relatively free of the administrative costs associated with other PLR systems. Nonetheless, it is a system most closely resembling social welfare, and "our political climate 'is not receptive to the introduction of new forms of social welfare.' "[46]

The higher costs of administering a system which tallies nationwide perhaps millions of transactions to determine fairly small payments to a relatively small number of persons is one reason to consider alternatives to public lending right,

> . . . other methods through which the importance of authorship could be recognized. . . . Libraries, for example, could pay augmented prices for books. . . . A more attractive idea was the exclusion of authors' royalties and fees from income taxation, at least up

> to a specified amount. This plan . . . avoids "pointing the finger" at libraries and would allow all authors to benefit, not just the authors of bestsellers and trade books. It would also avoid sampling and all its inherent difficulties.[47]

f. The Commission shall "*assess whether the eligibility of the author to receive compensation should be subject to specific limitations such as (i) the copyright status of the work; (ii) the nationality or domicile of the author; (iii) the alienability or descendability of the right to compensation; or (iv) a specified term of years.*"[48]

These seemingly peripheral legal issues surrounding public lending right proposals cut to the heart of the question of what the nature and purpose of PLR legislation is. For example, if the underlying premise of PLR is that it is additional protection of intellectual property needed because fundamental rights of ownership historically incorporated in copyright law have been effectively negated by library lending, then it follows PLR participation should continue for a work until the copyright expires and the work enters into the public domain. On the other hand, if the underlying premise is one of financial protection against lost royalties from sales, then PLR should be operative only so long as the author (or publisher) has any reasonable expectation of continued sales of a work (perhaps for a fixed number of years or for as long as the publisher has stock in print for sale). Or, if the underlying premise is one of cultural encouragement for writers, then PLR payments should continue for all works but only during the life of the author.

Not all PLR nations have addressed some of these issues; but where they have, the legislation seems irreconcilable to any consistent underlying principle. In the United Kingdom books can be registered for PLR only if the author applies during his lifetime. But once a book has been registered, the PLR interest in it continues for 50 years after the author's death. The PLR interest can be assigned and also can pass by will or intestate succession.[49] In short, the PLR interest attaches to the work (not to the author) but does so by virtue of registration (not by virtue of the work's creation).

In Denmark, Sweden and West Germany, the PLR interest cannot be assigned, but can be inherited. Ostensibly, the nonassignability of PLR payments is imposed to protect authors by preventing publishers from negotiating the payments as offsets against royalties in royalty agreements. Publishers do have a financial interest in library lending activities since profits from sales of books are affected in much the same way as authors' royalties are affected. And yet publishers are specifically excluded in public lending right schemes in Denmark, Finland, Iceland, The Netherlands, New Zealand, Norway and Sweden.[50] In Australia, a publishers' PLR provides 15 cents per estimated copy held in the public libraries. Australian publishers are eligible if, in the opinion of a PLR committee, they regularly publish books in the country.[51] In West Germany publishers receive PLR payments equal to 30 percent of the authors' payments.

The foregoing legal issues relating to duration, succession and assignability have generally developed after the basic concept of PLR has been debated. The legal issue centering on the PLR concept itself is the question whether public lending right is an element of copyright law:

> [I]n strict logic, an author should be rewarded by his publisher with a lump sum payment instead of a royalty, since his work is completed before a single copy can be sold. Additional sales do not involve him in additional work. The existence of the royalty system represents a compromise necessitated by uncertainty as to likely sales and hence the economic value of the author's work. On the other hand, it may imply a tacit acknowledgment by publishers or readers that the author is entitled to payment in relation to the satisfaction he provides for his readers. . . . This argument implies a notional link between lending right and copyright, though no copy of the publication is in fact made.[52]

The notional link is stronger than that. "Everyone has the right to the protection of the moral and material interests resulting from any scientific, literary or artistic production of which he is the author."[53] To protect this right, nations enact copyright laws, and they join together to ratify international copyright conventions "which are meant to internationalize the national protection of authors."[54] Thus, the Berne Convention for the Protection of Literary and Artistic Works provides that authors of the signatory nations enjoy the same "rights which their respective laws do now or may hereafter grant to their nationals."[55] The Universal Copyright Convention provides that nationals of the Contracting States "shall enjoy in each other Contracting State the same protection as that other State accords to works of its nationals first published in its own territory."[56] All eleven PLR countries are parties to both conventions, but only West Germany has enacted its public lending right scheme as part of its copyright statute. In the United Kingdom authors argued throughout the 1970s that public lending right was an extension of the fundamental right to protection of intellectual property and had nothing to do with welfare subsidies for writers. The resulting British act, however, is outside the Copyright Act.

> One might have assumed that the reluctance to pass PLR as part of the copyright act had stemmed from philosophical differences about the nature of copyright. . . . But this would have been an erroneous conclusion. . . .

> The real reason why all nations other than Great Britain [*sic.*, West Germany] decided to avoid inclusion of PLR in their respective copyright acts was to exclude foreigners from eligibility for payments. Since in all PLR countries the funds come directly out of governmental appropriations and not from users' fees paid by library patrons, none of those states saw any particular need to support foreign authors not resident in their countries.[57]

As noted, the British PLR scheme provides recognition to a foreign author if the United Kingdom and the foreign author's nation have a reciprocal agreement relating to PLR.

The Berne Convention and Universal Copyright Convention encompass only those national laws comprehended within the copyright acts, and whether public lending right is a right flowing from authorship to be protected by copyright is more than idle speculation. Some theorists, especially German scholars, contend that attempting to remove authors' protection from the umbrella of copyright law with separate PLR schemes is a violation of these international copyright treaties, and noncopyright PLR may be invalid.[58]

This monolithic view of the purview of copyright protection has merit at the level of abstraction that international jurists employ in the attempt to make sense of a less-than-consistent world of nations. At the national level, however, the abstract "bundle of rights" that protects authors and other creators of intellectual property shows considerable variation. In the civil law jurisdictions of continental Europe, for example, the bundles include the *droit moral* to protect the creator's continuing interests in preserving the artistic integrity of the work and the *droit de suite* to protect the creator's continuing economic interests in subsequent exploitation of the work. Both concepts are not yet widely recognized as part of the protection afforded intellectual property in common law jurisdictions such as the United States. The U.S. resistance to recognizing these concepts may in fact be one reason this country has not entered into the Berne Convention.[59]

In short, quite apart from the motive to exclude foreign authors from PLR eligibility, there may be other reasons why PLR schemes should not be within copyright which are firmly based in common law doctrine relating to the scope of copyright protection. In U.S. copyright law, for example, the principle of exhaustion is based on the idea that once a copy of the author's work is sold, the rights of the author in that physical object cease. Sale of the copy conveys no copyright interest to the buyer, but as to that copy, the buyer can resell, lend, donate, or destroy it at will. The author's interest in that copy is exhausted, and subsequent collective use of that copy through library lending does not override the principle. By this reasoning, PLR schemes are outside the law of copyright. In West Germany, the PLR statute within the copyright law is considered "a breach in the bulwark of the exhaustion theory."[60] Some countries, such as France, simply do not recognize the exhaustion principle.

Even in United States law, copyright protection already extends beyond the exhaustion principle in some areas. For example, the comprehensive Copyright Act of 1976 includes sections relating to compulsory licensing statutes (considered as part of *droit de suite* protection in continental Europe) which cover phonorecords, re-transmissions by cable television systems and jukeboxes.[61] "Essentially, a compulsory license is one conferred by statute . . . [which] enables others to use a copyright work, by copying, performing, displaying, or otherwise, without infringement when the user has fulfilled specified conditions, including the payment of royalties."[62] Compulsory licensing statutes already alter the exhaustion principle within copyright protection, and perhaps no new conceptual framework is needed to include compensation to authors in a similarly arranged PLR scheme.[63]

Despite the sharp delineation of the PLR-as-copyright issue encouraged by the broad contextual analysis of international treaty obligations or by the narrower view of national variations in acceptance of the exhaustion principle, there is no indication of how or when the problem will be resolved in the United States. Meanwhile, another significant legal issue relating to the import of *droit de suite* and *droit moral* civil law to the United States is being resolved, and the results do have a direct bearing on potential PLR development. That issue is whether, in the absence of federal legislation, individual states may enact *droit de suite* and *droit moral* laws.

California and New York are centers of artistic activities in the United States, and both have enacted legislation which extends economic and creative protection to artists beyond the copyright protection of federal law. In 1977 California enacted the Resale Royalties Act,[64] *droit de suite* legislation providing that whenever a work of fine art is sold, the seller must pay 5 percent of the sale price to the artist provided that the price exceeds $1,000, the seller is a State resident, or the sale is transacted in California, and the artist is alive. In 1979 the legislature followed with the California Art Preservation Act,[65] a *droit moral* statute that protects works of art from being defaced, mutilated, altered or destroyed. The New York legislature followed with its own *droit moral* measure in 1983—the Artist's Authorship Rights Act[66]—to prevent mutilation or alteration of works of fine art, including limited editions of photographs and sculptures, but excluding motion pictures and literary works.

In each instance the underlying issue is the same: are these statutes valid under the federal doctrine of preemption?[67] In the first court test of those statutes, *Morseburg v. Balyon*,[68] art dealers refused to pay the California artist royalty, arguing primarily that the federal Copyright Act preempted California law. Federal District Judge Takasugi disagreed by concluding that "[n]ot only does the California law not significantly impair any federal interest, but it is the very type of innovative lawmaking that our federalist system is designed to encourage."[69] Indeed, "New York and California have stepped in to plug a gap in protections for artists where Congress has failed to act and the theoretical underpinnings are so diverse."[70] The U.S. Constitution empowers Congress "To promote the Progress of Science and useful Arts, by securing for limited Times to Authors and Inventors the exclusive Right to their respective Writings and Discoveries."[71] If Congress does not exercise that power with regard to public lending right legislation, the *Morseburg* decision provides some precedent to suggest that states may enact their own PLR schemes in the United States. That would not be a preferred solution to author economic protection for library lending. Nonetheless, it may well be that "[s]tate legislation will encourage Congress to provide royalties for artists on the national level."[72]g. "*Within two years after its first meeting, the Commission shall submit to the President and to the Congress a final report which shall include its recommendations and its proposals, if any, for legislation and administrative action. . . .*"[73] Perhaps it is intentional that there is no charge to the Commission to determine if public lending right is a part of copyright law even though the bill's caption establishes the Commission to study the feasibility of amending the copyright laws. The issues of law, policy and administration could be debated endlessly, and clearly the bill intends to avoid that by setting a time limit for the Commission to conclude its work.

As Robert Caro has noted about the protracted debate in the United Kingdom that ultimately led to mistrust between writers and librarians: "It would be quite a waste if we had to go through the same dreary scenario in the U.S. Moreover, we shouldn't be fighting at all. We are all on the same side. We need to work together to develop a fair scheme for compensating authors for the multiple use of their copyrighted book in libraries."[74]

Nevertheless, managers of libraries and information services, particularly public funded ones, should familiarize themselves with the proposed PLR bill and should be sensitive to the issues it raises. If approved, the implications of PLR will be far reaching and serious to librarianship from the administrative/funding viewpoint. Awareness of the development of the bill is therefore necessary to all librarians.

NOTES

1. Goodman, William B., quoted in Cole, John Y., "Public Lending Right, A Symposium at the Library of Congress," Appendix to *Library of Congress Information Bulletin* 42:427 (December 12, 1983), at p. 428.

2. Income data taken from "Figure 3: 1979 Writing Related Income-Percentage Distribution of

Authors by Income Category," "The Columbia Economic Survey of American Authors; a Summary of Findings," *op. cit.*, at p. 1196.

3. Findlater, Richard, ed. *Public Lending Right: A Matter of Justice*. London: André Deutsch, 1971, at p. 11.

4. Seemann, *op. cit.*, at p. 81.

5. Nasri, William Z., "Public Lending Right: Fair or Welfare," *Journal of Library Administration* 6:7 (1985).

6. H.R. 4850, 93d Cong., 1st Sess. (1973).

7. S. 2192, 98th Cong., 1st Sess. (1983).

8. S. 658, 99th Cong., 1st Sess. (1985).

9. Dates given for initial passage of enabling legislation. *Cf.*, "Table 2 Public Lending Right Benefits in Ten Countries," in Seemann, *op. cit.* at p. 118; Nasri, *op. cit.*, at p. 7; Koch, Ole, "Situation in Countries of Continental Europe," in Perry Morrison and Dennis Hyatt, eds. "Public Lending Right," *Library Trends* 29:565 (1981), at p. 641. These authors, among others, may show differing dates based on the effective date of the Act, the date of implementation of administrative regulations or similar events. In the United Kingdom, for example, the 1979 enabling legislation did not result in the promulgation of administrative rules until 1982, and the first payments to authors under the British system were not made until January 1984 based on a sampling of library loans for 1983. In West Germany, Section 27 of the comprehensive revision of the copyright law in 1965 provided that copyright holders should receive reasonable compensation in instances where their works are rented for profit. A 1972 amendment to the act created a public lending right for not-for-profit lending. "In Denmark, a new law on PLR came into force as from January 1, 1983, separate from the law on public libraries. The scheme has been extended, but not changed radically." Letter, from Ole Koch, Assistant Director, State Inspection of Public Libraries, Copenhagen, Denmark, to John Y. Cole, Executive Director, The Center for the Book, Library of Congress, September 12, 1983. In Canada administrative regulations creating public lending right were promulgated in February 1986 under the name Payment for Public Use. Additional administrative regulations to implement the plan have not yet been developed, but $3,000,000 has been allocated for the fiscal year beginning April 1, 1986. "Initially the Canadian plan is expected to be based on library holdings rather than library loans." Mitgang, Herbert, "A Penny for Their Thoughts How Authors Can Get Library 'Royalties,' " *New York Times Book Review*, March 30, 1986, at p. 3.

10. Stave, Thomas, "Public Lending Right: A History of the Idea," in "Public Lending Right," *id.*, at p. 572.

11. S. 658, *op. cit.*, at Sec. 2.

12. Hyatt, Dennis, quoted in "Public Lending Right, A Symposium at the Library of Congress," *op. cit.*, at p. 430.

13. Astbury, Raymond, "The Situation in the United Kingdom," in "Public Lending Right," *op. cit.*, at p. 664.

14. Caro, Robert, in "Public Lending Right, A Symposium at the Library of Congress," *op. cit.*, at p. 428.

15. Remarks of George Piternick, Professor Emeritus, School of Librarianship, University of British Columbia, from the author's notes of the Public Lending Right Symposium at the Library of Congress, September 29, 1983.

16. Paul Goldstein, Professor of Law, Stanford University, from radio broadcast interview with Susan Stamberg, "All Things Considered," National Public Radio, October 9, 1983.

17. S. 658, *op. cit.*, at Sec. 2.

18. Lawrey, Keith, quoted in McCormick, Edith, "PLR Could Cost Libraries Millions, Fussy System Promises Few Pence for Authors As British Public Lending Right Begins," *American Libraries* 14:107 (February 1983).

19. Wedgeworth, Robert, in "Public Lending Right, A Symposium at the Library of Congress," *op. cit.*, at p. 429.

20. S. 658, *op. cit.*, at Sec. 3.

21. Schrader, Dorothy, in "Public Lending Right, A Symposium at the Library of Congress," *op. cit.*, at p. 428.

22. Library data compiled from "Table 10.6 – Public Libraries: Collections, Borrowers, Works Loaned Out, Current Expenditure, Personnel," *UNESCO Statistical Yearbook*, 1977: 774-781. Information reported in the table for 1974. The inclusion of West Germany with the six countries of

Norden Europe significantly dilutes the data. For example, Denmark has 6.43 library volumes per capita and 16.45 annual loan transactions per capita at one end of the statistical range while West Germany anchors the other end with .7 library volumes per capita and 2.18 annual loan transactions per capita.

23. Remarks of Robert Wedgeworth, from the author's notes of the Public Lending Right Symposium at the Library of Congress, September 29, 1983.

24. Wedgeworth, Robert, in "Public Lending Right, a Symposium at the Library of Congress," *op. cit.*, at p. 429.

25. Kirkegaard, Preben, "Author's Lending Right in Scandinavia," in *Proceedings of the Twenty-seventh Annual Conference,* Canadian Library Association. Ottawa: The Association, 1972, at p. 83.

26. *Id.*

27. Mason, Diana B., "PLR: Are We Willing to Support Canadian Talent?" *Canadian Library Journal* 32:427 (1975).

28. Dietz, Adolf, *Copyright Law in the European Community*. Alphen aan den Rijn, the Netherlands: Sijthoff & Noordhoff, 1978, at p. 14.

29. Sumsion, John W., quoted in "Public Lending Right, A Symposium at the Library of Congress," *op. cit.*, at p. 430.

30. S. 658, *op. cit.*

31. Sumsion, John W., in "Public Lending Right, A Symposium at the Library of Congress," *op. cit.*, at p. 430.

32. Wedgeworth, Robert, in "Public Lending Right, A Symposium at the Library of Congress," *op. cit.*, at p. 429.

33. "Public Lending Right," *Australian Book Scene 1983-84*, at p. 36.

34. "Information for Writers and Illustrators of Books," a brochure prepared by the Office of Public Lending Right, Bayheath House, Prince Regent Street, Stockton-On-Tees, Cleveland, England [undated].

35. Sumsion, John W., quoted in "Public Lending Right, A Symposium at the Library of Congress," *op. cit.*, at p. 430.

36. Astbury, Raymond, "Situation in the United Kingdom," in "Public Lending Right," *op. cit.*, at p. 679.

37. Sumsion, John W., "Public Lending Right, Registrar Describes How the Scheme Will Work," *Library Association Record* 84:243 (July/August 1982).

38. "Information for Writers and Illustrators of Books," *op. cit.*

39. May, Derwent, "Public Lending Right—If Your Book Was Borrowed Once, You Got £2," *The Listener* 111:10 (January 26, 1984).

40. "Information for Writers and Illustrators of Books," *op. cit.*

41. Trewin, Ion, "British Authors Get First PLR Royalties," *Publishers Weekly*, 225:31 (February 17, 1984).

42. *Id.*

43. S. 658, *op. cit.*, at sec. 2.

44. Sumsion, John W., *Setting Up Public Lending Right; A Report to the Advisory Committee September 1984*. Darlington: Marford Lithographic, 1984, at p. 18. In his report the Registrar notes that of the 649 million estimated loans in 1983, 182 million were made of books on the PLR Register. The remaining 72 percent of the loans related to books written by dead or foreign authors, to books that were ineligible, and to books where registration was not applied for. Based on a random selection of 918 books, Sumsion reports that the PLR paid to domestic authors would have been halved if books by foreign authors had been allowed. *Id.*

45. Koch, Ole, "The Situation in Continental Europe" in Public Lending Right," *op. cit.*, at p. 645.

46. Stave, Thomas, quoted in "Public Lending Right, A Symposium at the Library of Congress," *op. cit.*, at p. 428.

47. Piternick, George, in "Public Lending Right, A Symposium at the Library of Congress," *op. cit.*, at p. 431.

48. S. 658, *op. cit.*, at Sec. 2.

49. "Information for Writers and Illustrators of Books," *op. cit.*

50. Seemann, Ernest A., "Table 2: Public Lending Right Benefits in Ten Countries," in "A Look at the Public Lending Right," *op. cit.*, at pp. 118-119.

51. "Public Lending Right," *Australian Book Scene 1983-84, op. cit.*

52. Jones, Arthur, "Practical and Economic Considerations" in "Public Lending Right," *op. cit.*, at p. 598.

53. Universal Declaration of Human Rights, Art. 27(2), in *United Nations Bulletin* 6:6 (No. 1, January 1, 1949), at p. 8.

54. Seemann, Ernest A., "A Look at the Public Lending Right," *op. cit.*, at p. 94.

55. Berne Convention for the Protection of Literary and Artistic Works (Paris Text—July 24, 1971) Art. 1, Sec. 4, in Nimmer, Melville B., *Nimmer on Copyright, A Treatise on the Law of Literary, Musical and Artistic Property, and the Protection of Ideas*. New York: Matthew Bender, 1985, at v. 4, appendix 27.

56. Universal Copyright Convention (Paris Text—July 24, 1971), Art. II, Sec. 1. *United States Treaties and Other International Agreements* 25, p. 2: 1343, at p. 1345, TIAS 7868.

57. Seemann, Ernest A., "A Look a the Public Lending Right"; *op. cit.*, at pp. 91-93.

58. *Id.*, at p. 95.

59. Nimmer, Melville, B., "Implications of the Prospective Revisions of the Berne Convention and the United States Copyright Law," *Stanford Law Review* 19:499 (1976), at p. 518. For possible reasons the United States has been reluctant to adopt these concepts, *see* Merryman, John H., "The Refrigerator of Bernard Buffet," *Hastings Law Journal* 27:1023 (1976), at p. 1042 (law in this area has not yet responded to social and cultural changes, such as the recent international recognition of American art); Katz, Arthur S., "The Doctrine of Moral Right and American Copyright Law—a Proposal," *Southern California Law Review*, 24:375 (1951), at p. 410 (the unwillingness of courts and legislatures to take responsibility for change: "They have not seen the doctrine in the light of a stimulating challenge, but as a threat, though ill-defined, to the *status quo* of copyright principle."). The United Kingdom is a signatory to the Berne Convention but has given little more than tacit recognition to the *droit moral* and *droit de suite*. The United States is a signatory to the Universal Copyright Convention which makes provision only in minor areas for protecting rights associated with *droit moral* or *droit de suite*.

60. Seemann, Ernest A., "A Look at the Public Lending Right," *op. cit.*, at p. 97.

61. Copyright Act of 1976, 17 *U.S. Code* §§111, 115, 116.

62. *Copyright Law Reporter*. Chicago: Commerce Clearing House, 1980, ¶3005 (looseleaf).

63. Hyatt, Dennis, "Legal Aspects of Public Lending Right," in "Public Lending Right," *op. cit.*, at p. 589.

64. California Civil Code, §986 (West, 1986 Supp.). A 1982 amendment to the California Act permits the resale royalties to be assigned and inherited.

65. California Civil Code, §987 (West, 1986 Supp.).

66. New York Arts & Cultural Affairs §14.03, *McKinney's Consolidated Laws of New York* (West, 1986 Supp.).

67. For discussion, *see* Francione, G.L., "The California Art Preservation Act and Federal Preemption by the 1976 Copyright Act—Equivalence and Actual Conflict," *Copyright Law Symposium* 31:105 (1984); Lubic, Douglas W., "New York Artists' Authorship Rights Act Incorporates European Moral Right Doctrine," *Fordham International Law Journal* 8:362 (1984-85).

68. *Morseburg v. Balyon*, 201 *U.S. Patents Quarterly* 518 (C.D. Cal. 1978), *aff'd* 621 F.2d 972 (9th Cir. 1980).

69. *Id.*, at p. 520.

70. Taubman, Joseph, "New York Artists' Authorship Rights of 1983: Waiver and Fair Use," *Cardozo Arts & Entertainment Law Journal* 3:113, at p. 122.

71. U.S. Constitution, Art. I, §8.

72. Green, Allan, *Royalties for Artists*. Salem, Oregon: Legislative Administration Committee, 1979, at p. 4.

73. S. 658, at sec. 7.

74. Caro, Robert, quoted in "Public Lending Right, A Symposium at the Library of Congress," *op. cit.*, at p. 428.

Professional Liability

William Z. Nasri

Liability is a legal term that includes almost any obligation, responsibility or duty that might arise as a result of a statute, a contract or tort. For example, Members of the Board of Directors of a corporation or a non-profit making organization are individually liable, under certain statutes, for decisions made in exercising their fiduciary duties. When based on contractual agreements, liability is a result of a breach of contract. On the other hand, liability which is based on tort is a result of a breach of duty such as liability for damages resulting from a car accident. The breached duty might be the care in driving the car which caused the damages.

The question may arise as to the reason for discussing liability in general and professional liability in particular in relation to library and information managers. In fact many such managers are likely to say that it will never happen to them. The question, therefore, is whether professional liability is a rhetorical supposition or a real possibility for library and information managers. The issue deserves consideration, primarily because of the potential harm an information professional might cause if he/she is not careful about, for example, how far he/she helps with reference service and/or readers advice.

Clientele come to a library or an information center for information and professional service. They usually accept what an information professional tells them as an accurate statement of fact. Therefore, if the advice proves to be faulty, the client may recover for injuries suffered as a result of the advice taken by suing for professional liability or malpractice the practitioner and, most likely, the library's director and board.

Professional liability/malpractice may be defined as any professional misconduct or unreasonable lack of skill in the performance of professional duties through intentional carelessness or simple ignorance. Thus, one has to assume that a professional person must be a responsible indi-

---

William Z. Nasri, JD, PhD (Pittsburgh), is a professor at the School of Library and Information Science, University of Pittsburgh, and the Coordinator of the Management of the Library and Information Services' area in the Department of Library Science. He serves also as a Copyright Consultant to the same University and to several other institutions. He is a writer and a national speaker on the legal issues involved in library and information management and he lectures annually at the Library Administrators Development Program at the University of Maryland. He is PLA Liaison to ALA Ad Hoc Committee on Copyright and he has served for several years on the Advisory Board of the Copyright Clearance Center.

vidual. Responsibility here is synonymous with accountability. Professionals are accountable for their behavior as well as for their professional knowledge and skill. Malpractice, therefore, is a professional disease one is liable to catch if one does not adhere to a certain standard of care in his/her professional activities.

One may ask, "Are librarians and information experts, professionals?" The answer, in essence, depends on the characteristics that make any profession. A profession is an occupation characterized by unique, definite, and recognized social service with an emphasis upon the intellectual techniques for performing this service. It involves a long period of education and training. It also affords the practitioner a broad range of autonomy balanced by personal responsibility for judgments made and acts performed within the scope of this autonomy. It emphasizes the service rendered rather than the economic gain to the practitioner. Finally, professions invariably have self-governing organizations and codes of ethics. All these characteristics suggest principles and issues to be considered in professional training, which in turn lead to competency.

Considering the previously mentioned characteristics, the author believes that librarians and information handlers, in general, are professionals. In fact, society is becoming more information oriented and information professionals are providing and will continue to provide a unique service which is increasingly being recognized as such. This role is intensifying and is becoming more apparent as time goes by.

As professionals, our daily activities and advice are based on certain knowledge and judgment on our part. Therefore, one has to assume that an information professional is well versed in his/her subject specialty; in the users' needs; and in the literature in his/her field of interest. One has to assume also that he/she is competent enough to advise those users and know what to recommend to them in their attempt at making decisions in their varied endeavors. The question is, "What if the librarian's or information specialist's advice is not the best?" In this case the user's decision, based on either's advice, will be faulty and damage may occur.

Recently professional liability/malpractice cases have been a rising tide. Successful claims against attorneys, for example, have increased by 35% in the last five years, and the upward trend is continuing. This has affected the legal practice insurance and its premium. It is estimated that over 75% of all practicing attorneys are now carrying malpractice insurance, compared to 10% twenty years ago. It has also affected some lawyers' advice, acts, and decisions. Preoccupied by the threat of being sued, some have become more conservative in their practice and noncommittal in their advice. An analogy can easily be drawn. With the proliferation of databases and files in almost every aspect of our public and private sectors and with the increased reliance on information in decision-making, the author cannot help but feel that one day an angry user may very well react to wrong information or poor advice, particularly if such advice and the reliance on it results in loss of money, opportunity, and/or advantages.

One may say that no librarian or information specialist has been sued for malpractice. The reason, in the author's opinion, is largely based on the fact that, as it stands, we are not collectible. But with the prospect of more reliance on information and with institutions, corporations, and networks being formed to handle and provide information, the possibility does exist. The fact that librarians and information specialists have not been sued to date does not negate their liability.

The recent rise in malpractice suits is said to be based on consumerism. People are more educated about their rights and the fulfillment of their expectations, particularly when they pay, directly or indirectly, for the services required. In addition, users and/or consumers are becoming more aware of the existence of incompetent professionals. Practitioners, on the other hand, are becoming aware also of the incompetency of some of their colleagues and are more apt to be outraged and willing to testify to it in court. Their testimony is out of both self-respect and self-preservation.

The court is contributing also to the incentive to sue professionals by expanding the scope of professional liability and insisting that any profession must conform, in matters of negligence, to other occupational groups. The court expects that "a professional must exercise such skill, prudence and diligence as professionals of ordinary skills and capacity commonly possess and exercise." "Skill" means that the professional practitioner must possess the knowledge of those plain and elementary principles in his/her profession which are commonly known by well-informed practitioners. "Prudence" means that the practitioner must make an informed decision based on an intelligent assessment of the question posed to him/her. Finally, "diligence" means that the practitioner must discover those additional rules which, although not commonly known, may readily be found by reasonable research techniques. It appears that a potential expansion of liability for professional malpractice into library and information services might not be far-fetched and should be of concern to practitioners and to information services' administrators.

One may ask, "Who is liable for inaccurate information or advice which is given to users?" Actually, the person who provides the information is liable for the harm caused by it. In the meantime, the director of the library or information services who employs the said person is jointly liable. This is based on the fact that employers are generally held responsible for acts committed by their employees within the scope of employment, even when the employee has been instructed not to act as he/she did. The library board of directors/trustees may also be held liable in the absence of sovereign or charitable immunity. Boards usually are sued in malpractice suits because they are the most likely defendant to have the money to pay damages.

What might a librarian/information specialist do to protect him/herself and thus protect the library or information center? A librarian/information specialist should keep the user aware of the status of the search in response to the user's request for information. It would be advisable for example, the library staff member to indicate to the user the type of sources at hand that the staff member has examined in his/her effort to find the needed information. An impression of a definite and comprehensive answer may build up false expectations and may lead to a malpractice suit. The professional staff member should also be alert to the performance of his/her subordinates. An information professional should make certain that juniors and nonprofessional staff members for whom he/she is responsible are well trained and efficient. Delegation of authority does not mean abdication of responsibility. Supervision of subordinates performance and output is, therefore, essential. Information professionals should also keep abreast of the literature in their fields of interest. Current awareness of what is involved in these fields is imperative. Likewise, professionals and their staff members should make every effort to attend appropriate conferences and continuing education activities in order to update their knowledge and to interact with colleagues. Consequently, information professionals should not accept problems in areas in which they are not fully competent. It is advisable for the librarian to refer the client to other libraries and/or sources which may be better equipped to handle the problem. Information professionals should not leave the client with the impression that they know when in fact they do not.

Information professionals should also take the time to verify their findings before transmitting them to the client. Reference to the sources of information is important. Finally, it behooves librarians and information specialists to keep a record of their activities and the steps taken in their search. This may be easier said than done. However, a record of a certain event may spell the difference between refuting or not refuting an unfounded claim of malpractice.

Another relatively recent method of safeguard against professional liability is to insure against damages which the practitioner might incur. Under such policy, the professional/policy holder pays premiums to the insurance company which in turn agrees to pay on behalf of the insured, damages occurring because of errors or mistakes in rendering professional services. Payment usually is up to, but does not exceed the limit set forth in any particular policy. A professional however, must be aware of the fact that such policies do not cover any damages arising from a breach of contract (such as a contract with a user of an information system).

Furthermore, this type of policy does not cover any damages arising outside the scope of one's profession. Consequently, there is no coverage for damages resulting from nonprofessional acts, such as closing a library's door on a user's hand. Therefore, it is advisable, for the information professional to read carefully the coverage clauses and the exclusions in any liability policy and to become fully aware of what liability the policy covers and what it excludes.

Finally, the author is of the opinion that the information profession must make renewed efforts towards improving the competency of the professional practitioner. This might be done through the educational and training process in addition to tougher screening, before allowing "information handlers" to practice. The profession should police itself, otherwise it may suffer unpleasant and increasingly likely consequences.

REFERENCES

Angoff, Allan, "Library Malpractice Suite: Could It Happen To You," *American Libraries*, Vol. 7, No. 8, September 1976, p. 489.

Brown, Thomas P. III, "Protect Yourself! It's Later Than You Think: Collective Efforts Toward Solution of Malpractice Problems (Part III)," *Oklahoma Bar Journal*, Vol. 51, May 31, 1980, pp. 1325-1329.

Chandler, "Computer Transactions: Potential Liability of Computer Users and Vendors," *Washington University Law Quarterly*, Vol. 77, 1977, p. 405.

DeRensis, Paul R., "The Impact of Computers on Professional Malpractice Liability," *Case and Comment*, Vol. 85, No. 3, May-June 1980, pp. 27-32.

Gambert v. Hart, 44 Cal. 542 (1972). Also Smith v. Lewis, 13 Cal. 3rd, p. 349, (1975).

Gillen, Dennis L., "Legal Malpractice," *Washburn Law Journal*, Vol. 12, No. 3, 1973, pp. 281-296.

Harper, F. and James, F., *The Law of Torts*, Little, Brown & Co., 1956, pp. 1374-1410, 1607-1627 and 1667-1675.

Hilliker, Donald B., "Malpractice in the 80's," *Barrister*, Vol. 7, Fall 1980, p. 116(7).

Leone, Gerome, "Malpractice Liability of a Law Librarian?" *Law Library Journal*, Vol. 73, No. 1, Winter 1980, pp. 46-65.

"Liability for Programming Errors," (Report on the Berlin Conference, August 1980) *International Business Law*, Vol. 9, July/August 1981, p. 303.

Lieberman, Myron, "Principles of Educational Preparation," in *Library Education: An International Survey*. Larry Bone, ed., (University of Illinois, 1968), pp. 153-154.

Maller, Ronald E., "Attorney's Liability for Errors of Judgment – At the Crossroads," *Tennessee Law Review*, Vol. 48, No. 2, Winter 1981, pp. 283-321.

Marke, Julius J., "The Librarian and You. Are You Missing the Boat?" *New York State Bar Journal*, Vol. 40 (1968), p. 344.

Mills, R. K., "Reference Service vs Legal Advice: Is It Possible to Draw the Line?" *Law Library Journal*, Vol. 72 (1979), p. 192.

Mills, Robin K., "Reference Service vs Legal Advice," *Law Library Journal*, Vol. 72 (1979), pp. 179-193.

Mintz, Anne P., "Information Practice and Malpractice: Do We Need Malpractice Insurance?" *Online*, Vol. 8, no. 4, July 1984, pp. 20-26.

Postema, Gerald J., "Moral Responsibility in Professional Ethics," *New York University Law Review*, Vol. 55, April 1980, pp. 63-89.

Schnidman, Richard J. and Mark J. Sulzher, "Legal Malpractice Dilemma," *Cincinnati Law Review*, Vol. 45, no. 4 (1976), p. 543.

Vandall, Frank J., "Applying Strict Liability to Professionals: Economic and Legal Analysis," *Indiana Law Journal*, Vol. 59, Winter 1984, pp. 25-64.

[illegible] Journal, Vol. [illegible] (1975), p. 94.

[illegible] Law Journal, Vol. [illegible] (1970), pp. 79-[illegible].

[illegible] Information Problems and Misapplied [illegible] Law Rev., Vol. [illegible] 1981, pp. 29-[illegible].

[illegible] "Moral Responsibility in Professions [illegible]" New York University Law Review, Vol. [illegible] 1980, pp. 63-79.

[illegible] "Malpractice Dilemma [illegible]" Vol. 45, [illegible] (1976), p. [illegible].

[illegible], Frank [illegible] "Applying Strict Liability to Professionals: Economic and Legal Analysis," [illegible] Law Journal, Vol. 59, Winter 1984, pp. 25-64.